VALUE
INVESTING
TODAY

VALUE INVESTING TODAY

CHARLES H. BRANDES

Second Edition

McGraw-Hill
New York • San Francisco • Washington, D.C.
Auckland • Bogotá • Caracas • Lisbon • London
Madrid • Mexico City • Milan • Montreal • New Delhi
San Juan • Singapore • Sydney • Tokyo • Toronto

Library of Congress Cataloging-in-Publication Data

Brandes, Charles H.
  Value investing today / Charles H. Brandes. — 2nd ed.
      p.   cm.
  Includes bibliographical references and index.
  ISBN 0-07-007190-X
  1. Stocks.   2. Investments   I. Title.
HG4661.B68   1997
332.67 ' 8—dc21   97-26016
                                                                CIP

McGraw-Hill

*A Division of The **McGraw·Hill** Companies*

1 2 3 4 5 6 7 8 9 0 DOC/DOC 9 0 2 1 0 9 8 7

ISBN 0-07-007190-X

The sponsoring editor for this book was Steven Sheehan, the editing
supervisor was Donna Namorato, and the production supervisor was
Suzanne W. B. Rapcavage. It was set in Palatino by Carol Graphics.

Printed and bound by R. R. Donnelley & Sons Company.

This publication is designed to provide accurate and authoritative
information in regard to the subject matter covered. It is sold with the
understanding that neither the author nor the publisher is engaged in
rendering legal, accounting, or other professional service. If legal advice or
other expert assistance is required, the services of a competent
professional person should be sought.

*—From a Declaration of Principles jointly adopted by a Committee of the
American Bar Association and a Committee of Publishers.*

McGraw-Hill books are available at special quantity discounts to use as
premiums and sales promotions, or for use in corporate training
programs. For more information, please write to the Director of Special
Sales, McGraw-Hill, 11 West 19th Street, New York, NY 10011. Or contact
your local bookstore.

 This book is printed on recycled, acid-free paper containing a
minimum of 50% recycled de-inked fiber.

To L. F. B.

CONTENTS

PREFACE

This is the second edition of a book first written and published in 1989. The fundamental value principles have changed very little since that time. In fact, the basics have been in place since 1934, when Benjamin Graham's landmark book, *Security Analysis,* was first published.

Today, however, a dynamic and changing world requires a discussion of value investing in the context of recent history. We now have a global investment scene of gigantic proportions. The world equity market has grown from $1.1 trillion in 1973 to over $19 trillion today. The amount of technological change has been phenomenal, and the pace of that change is accelerating. Free enterprise and capitalism are expanding around the world. Free trade principles are increasingly being accepted as sound policy, and emerging markets are growing quickly. Since the 1930s, a better understanding of capitalism and economies has resulted in significant improvements in the economic well-being of people around the globe. And managerial skill has improved on the corporate and organizational levels.

This book discusses the implications of these and other changes for value investors. The potential for conservative and businesslike value investors has never been greater. In recognition of the spectacular growth in opportunities for successful value investing abroad, this edition expands the analysis of global equity markets. Accounting principles in foreign countries also are covered in considerable detail.

Many people helped with the production of this edition. I gratefully acknowledge their contributions.

Colleagues at our investment firm have been of great assistance. Managing Partner Glenn Carlson, CFA, was especially helpful in expanding Part 3 on international investing. Glenn's knowledge of the essence of worldwide value investing is clear and precise. Our other portfolio managers, whose knowledge of accounting principles and foreign countries is extensive, also contributed much to these parts of the book. Thank you all.

A true professional, Mr. Tom Saler, was instrumental for his writing ability, editorial assistance, research, and timely work. Thank you, Tom. Of course, any editorial problems and errors in research are mine.

Finally, I am greatly indebted to my mentor, "The Dean of Investing," Mr. Benjamin Graham. His basic principles formed the solid foundations for my worldwide investment success.

INTRODUCTION

Once upon a time there was an emperor with no clothes. His loyal subjects overlooked this deficiency until one child, casting aside convention and social custom, proclaimed the truth—the emperor wasn't all he seemed to be.

If you've been involved in the financial world and if you've stood back and observed its machinations thoughtfully, you'll have noticed that there have been many naked emperors. Doubtless, there will be many more.

There is no question that some people will make substantial money by investing in stocks. Others, like the emperor, will lose their shirts. This book is directed toward those investors who know that the worthwhile things in life have to be earned, toward the people who know that quick fixes are likely to be no fixes at all.

The main purpose of this book, then, is to help you take advantage of true investment opportunities by supplying you with the principles of the most successful means of investing over the past 60 years—value investing. I will admit to being a convert to this approach and, as with many converts, I am deeply committed to it. I have seen the results; I know it works; and I know it will build wealth for those who apply its principles.

A QUICK TOUR

Never before has a book of this nature been so important. Think not? Perhaps a short tour of our investing arena will change your mind.

For several years now, some individual investors have shaken off the trammels of reason. Instead, they have opted to run wild after golden visions, turning to fads, alchemy, and the stars and moon in desperate efforts to increase their wealth.

Consider the 1960s. Visions of boundless wealth floated before investors with the advent of a new magic formula: *synergy*. Synergy meant that under astute corporate management two and two could indeed equal five.

Synergy was not the first—nor the last—of such gimmicks. We've had go-go stocks, the high-turnover performance game, guessing market cycles and turns, technical analysis, and an infatuation with high technology and new issues. We also have seen the good company/bad price syndrome reappear, as it did in the 1970s, when the so-called nifty-fifty stocks sold at price/earnings ratios that reached the sky. During the 1990s, momentum investing—the notion of buying stocks simply because they were going up—became popular. What each of these fads has in common is a complete disregard for fundamental value.

FUNNY MONEY GAMES COME BACK TO LIFE

In the 1980s, we saw the reemergence of the old funny-money game of the public utility holding companies—financial entrepreneurs using good businesses, such as food companies with established brands, as the base for capital structures so weak as to leave no margin for safety, even for bondholders. We again watched investors exchange stocks at a rate as costly as it is pointless.

More recently we've had the high debt and junk bond phenomenon. Although different, it is still an approach totally lacking in reason and in a sense of history. But in perhaps the ultimate example of unreasonable and historically myopic behavior, in 1996 we witnessed the spectacle of investors elbowing one another for the chance to pay $40 and $50 a share for stocks of companies with no earnings and no prospects for earnings this century. Six months after the buying frenzy began, the speculative price bubble in the initial public offering market burst, sobriety returned, and badly burned individuals had learned the painful lesson that, once again, it wasn't different this time.

Sophisticated investors may snort P. T. Barnum-like remarks directed toward the gullibility of amateur investors and their capricious attitude, but they would be wrong. Amateur investors aren't the only ones at fault. The best and brightest financial professionals have proven equally gullible. Many pension funds, for example, judge the performance of their money managers on a quarterly basis. Inevitably, this forces managers to chase what's hot and disregard sound value principles. In fact, the IPO bubble of '96 was as much a product of institutional excesses as of the mistakes of their odd-lot counterparts.

Pension funds, insurance companies, and other institutional investors have indeed been abandoning any notion of making a painstaking analysis of the companies whose stocks they buy.[1] Almost uniformly, a variety of strategies have been adopted that may differ in some respects but have one horrendous defect in common: They all reject the need or feasibility of making company-by-company judgments about price and value or the need to examine time horizons or other factors that have some relation to the basic fundamentals necessary for long-term investing.

SHORT-TERM THINKING NOW IN VOGUE

Near-frenzied trading currently engulfs the securities markets. They have been turned into senior-level Las Vegases. Investors come and go with dazzling frequency. Each of them strives for a larger share of the average annual gains pie; each strives to speed up the process of wealth building. Instead, however, they find themselves switching in and out of stocks, feeding the brokers instead of themselves.

We have become increasingly preoccupied with short-term events and short-term results. A national impatience has gripped our lives, a trend exacerbated by the gusher of seemingly endless profits flowing from the long-term bull market in stocks which began in August 1982.

To borrow a few words from Sir John Templeton, a global money manager, there is too much emphasis now in America on everything yesterday. We are no longer as thrifty as we should be, and this is leading to more speculation, more danger, and more risk. Most American investors look too much at the short term, because they think it is so simple to make a right decision that all you need to know is which company is going to have good earnings next year. But it is not as easy as that. As our expectations have increased, our ability to wait and anticipate has decreased. The attention span of most Americans today is about the length of a television show.[2]

This fact applies equally well to the financial world. In Lewis Carroll's classic, *Through the Looking-Glass,* Humpty-Dumpty says that words mean exactly what he wants them to mean.

Keep this in mind the next time you visit the New York Stock Exchange (NYSE) and listen to the recorded message it has on hand. The message informs us that "investment objectives have changed from quick-dollar schemes to savings-oriented vehicles concerned with long-term security."[3] Have they? Consider that during 1996 at the NYSE, 105 billion shares switched owners, or 59.2 percent of all stock outstanding. Another 138 billion shares were traded on the NASDAQ stock market. Add these to the billions traded on the American and regional exchanges.

If stocks are a good long-term investment, why aren't they held longer? One explanation lies in the mixed messages investors receive from professionals and the financial media alike. In one breath, investors are advised to stay the course and to hang on for the long haul. In the next breath they are given a road map to short-term riches, plausible-sounding guides to switch around and chase the latest fad.

Evidence suggests that most are doing the latter. One recent study found that the average holding period for individuals invested in no-load, growth-oriented mutual funds was a meager 17 months.[4] If investors are to make money consistently, what is required is a return to far-sighted, long-term investing. That is the only kind of investing that promises rational investors the greatest economic rewards over the long haul.

WHAT IS MEANT BY INVESTING? BY SPECULATING?

Since the investing world currently seems stuck with Alice in Wonderland definitions, what is meant by investing? By speculation?

The distinction between investing and speculation has always been difficult to define, even though we understand it well enough in familiar terms. As one turn-of-the-century commentator noted, when a "security is bought and paid for in full, put away in a place of safe keeping, and held for the income it produces—that is called an investment." But, when it "is held for sale as soon as the price advances—that is speculation."[5] I would add: (1) any contemplated holding period shorter than a normal business cycle (three to five years) is speculation, and (2) any purchase based on anticipated market movements or forecasting is also speculation.

Investors and speculators approach their tasks differently. Investors want to know what a business is worth and imagine themselves as owning the business as a whole. Speculators are less interested in what a business is actually worth and more concerned with what a third party will pay to own shares on a given day.

But who can tell what a third party will pay for your shares today, tomorrow, or any day? Markets typically swing between extremes of fear and greed; both are irrational emotions, beyond anyone's ability to forecast. Evidence suggests that those who try—known as market "timers"—usually fail. One study of 100 large pension funds found "that while all the funds had engaged in at least some market timing, not one of the funds had improved its rate of return as a result of its efforts at timing. In fact, 89 of the 100 lost as a result of 'timing'—and their losses averaged a daunting 4.5 percent over the five-year period." The study concluded, "The evidence suggests strongly that mutual funds as a group are not successful at market timing activities. We believe the same would hold true for other groups of institutional investors, measured as a whole."[6]

Now consider the price tag for trying and failing to correctly time the market. According to a study by Ibbotson Associates, if you had put $1 into the average large-company stock in January 1926, your investment would have grown to $1,114 by year-end 1995. But if you had missed the 35 best months over those 70 years, your return would have dropped to just $10.16, or 109 times less.[7]

This completes our tour. As you can see, a return to proper investing methods today is important—no, vital. You will find those methods outlined in *Value Investing Today.*

SUCCESS DEPENDS ON THREE FACTORS

First, let us look at the basic ingredients necessary for your investing success. As with any endeavor, success depends on three key factors: knowledge, correct action, and patience.

This book supplies the necessary knowledge to guide you toward investments that will help protect and enhance your capital in today's radically changing world. Because of the lightening pace of financial change in the past few years, such a guide is more important now than ever before.

I also spoke of two other key factors: correct action and patience. These you must supply yourself.

The bottom line of value investing, of course, is to make money. If you use the value-investing approach and related tools suggested in the following pages, you should increase your capital, possibly substantially.

ONLY IF THE PRICE IS RIGHT

Value investing was already enjoying the finest pedigree of any investment strategy when I first learned of it in the early 1970s. At that time, I was privileged to become an acquaintance of one of the great financial legends of our time, Benjamin Graham.

Graham, together with another Columbia University professor, David Dodd, first set forth value-investing principles in their 778-page epic, *Security Analysis*. Although modified many times over the ensuing decades, the essential concept of value investing remains unchanged: The shares of any sound company—even a boring, slow-growing business—are a fine investment if bought at a cheap enough price.

Graham was value investing's leading prophet, but he was more than that. He transformed investing from an art form based mainly on Wall Street blather—imagination, guesswork, and inside information—into a methodical discipline. Graham believed that any conscientious investor could map a high trail through the slough of market fluctuations by paying close attention to investment fundamentals and by taking advantage of undervaluation and mispricing of individual securities.

Has value investing paid off? Yes, and I'll elaborate on and document that success in Chapter 1. In fact, value principles are justifying themselves even more thoroughly now than ever before.

Graham's philosophy was much akin to that of financier Bernard Baruch, who, writing of the 1929 stock market crash, said: "I have always thought that if ... even in the very presence of dizzily spiraling stock prices, we had all continuously repeated *two and two still makes four,* much of the evil might have been averted."[8] In other words: Fundamentals. Fundamentals. Fundamentals.

RECOGNIZED TODAY BY LIP SERVICE

Oddly enough, Wall Street respected Graham but never totally embraced his philosophy—paying lip service, instead. For many, value investing is too painstaking, too boring, and too disciplined. Few will stay the course, since there is no excitement, no action in watching eggs that take years to come to a boil. Value investing strains too much the patience and will of the investor, who needs courage to play against the crowd—often under trying circumstances.

REASONS FOR THIS BOOK

This book is important for several reasons. The first is the need to remind investors that patience is necessary if large and enduring profits are to be made from equity investments. Put another way, it is often easier to tell what will happen to the price of a security than *when* it will happen.

The second reason is the need to redirect investor thinking. The stock market is inherently misleading. Doing what everybody else is doing can often be wrong.

Third, the globalization of economies and markets has created new arenas in which to apply value principles. Fully two-thirds of the world's businesses are now domiciled outside the United States. As successful as value investing has been domestically, evidence suggests that it is even more effective overseas. That's because many foreign-based portfolio managers are "top-down" in their securities selection process. In other words, they make buy-and-sell decisions based on their outlook for a given market as a whole, rather than on the fundamental values of individual companies. For the value investor, this means less competition for global stocks and greater opportunities to buy at bargain-basement prices. In addition to enhancing return, applying value principals to foreign markets helps lower risk by increasing a portfolio's diversification.

Finally, American investors today have many financial alternatives that were not around—or effectually available—during Graham's time. It is important to address several of these issues as well in light of Graham's principles.

There is one group in particular I believe could benefit from this book—smaller investors with some experience in the market. In other words, *Value Investing Today* was not designed as a how-to book for total novices or as a textbook for highly skilled professionals. It should provide valuable assistance, however, to small investors who've taken the first few steps. I've spoken with many of these people and have noted that some have picked up all sorts of investment ideas and notions that could prove expensive.

So, *Value Investing Today* addresses a philosophy and strategy that will help small investors be more successful. As you go through the book's pages, you'll discover sound methods of fact gathering and interpretation, and begin to appreciate the need for discipline and patience.

Another point to consider: When I've talked with small investors, the most striking feature has been their tendency to set sail on financial oceans without so much as a chart to guide them. In *Value Investing Today*, you will find a way to design and implement a conservative and effective investment philosophy. It is a philosophy, I would emphasize, that already has proven to be a successful means of building wealth and conserving capital.

NOTES

1. Louis Lowenstein, *What's Wrong with Wall Street* (New York: Addison-Wesley Publishing, 1988), p. 1.

2. John Templeton, "Advertisement for Shearson Lehman Hutton," *New York Times Magazine,* October 23, 1988.

3. John Rothchild, *A Fool and His Money* (New York: Viking-Penguin, 1988).

4. Brandes Bulletin, Winter 1994-95, citing a study by Dalbar Financial Services.

5. Sereno S. Pratt, *The Work of Wall Street* (New York: Appleton, 1903).

6. Jerome B. Cohen, Edward D. Zinbarg, and Arthur Zeikel, *Investment Analysis and Portfolio Management* (Homewood, IL: Irwin, 1987).

7. Ibbotson Associates, Chicago, Illinois.

8. Charles Mackay, *Extraordinary Popular Delusions and the Madness of Crowds* (New York: Crown Publishers, 1932), Foreword, p. xiv.

VALUE INVESTING TODAY

WHY VALUE INVESTING MAKES DOLLARS AND SENSE

1

CHAPTER

Rewards of Value Investing

Sometimes investing seems easy. If you had purchased $10,000 worth of common shares of Xerox in 1960, your investment would have been worth $16.5 million in 1970. Suppose in 1982 you had put an extra $1,000 into shares of the Price Company. Cashing out in 1986 would have returned a heady $18,000.

That, of course, encapsulates the American dream: finding a "gee-whiz" stock that offers a spectacular run and a shortcut to wealth. Everyone has heard of someone who presently sails his new yacht off the coast of Mexico, thanks to the purchase of Genentech or Intel shares at just the right time. Unfortunately, such examples prove rare for most investors. For them the path, at best, has been full of gravel.

Even so, certain investors are obtaining superior results, watching their portfolios grow, taking some profits, and encountering minimal risk, year in, year out.

How? Not by listening to innumerable prophets, the ones that spring up during bad times with "new" strategies and advice. Nor by employing complicated theories such as market timing, efficient market, or asset allocation—in fact, any of the intricate tools of academicians or market technicians. (The IRS rarely receives estate tax windfalls from market technicians who have generated superior rates of return *over the long haul*.) And certainly not by happenchance or accident. These investors' goals are being accomplished instead by doing it the old-fashioned way—through value investing.

The purpose of this chapter is to review the rewards of value investing. Actual records of professional money managers, as well as results from performance studies, are presented. The reader should keep in mind that value investing is not a get-rich-quick scheme or an investment panacea. Don't expect home runs. By carefully following its principles, however, prudent, rational investors may obtain four significant advantages.

FOUR BENEFITS OF VALUE INVESTING

The first benefit of value investing is that it lowers your risk, especially compared to pure growth or other strategies. Value investing is almost synonymous with capital preservation. Conversely, growth investors are subject to large permanent declines.

The second benefit is lower portfolio volatility. Even though a portfolio's *aggregate* value may fluctuate, the chapters ahead will demonstrate why that should not concern the average investor.

The third benefit is reduced trading costs. Since value proponents hold securities for extended periods, buying and selling costs are cut. The savings go to the patient investor.

The fourth benefit is more pragmatic—the pot of gold. The bottom line is that value investing pays off in dollars and cents.

A Matter of Style

There are many variations of investment management, but two general styles predominate: value and growth. These distinctions can be confusing, since both strategies seek *growth of principal* as their primary objective. But that's where the similarity ends.

Growth-oriented managers buy the stocks of companies whose profits are expected to increase rapidly. Industries where growth stocks might be concentrated include beverages, health care, pharmaceuticals, household nondurables, and technology.

Value-oriented managers typically own the stocks of companies which are cheap relative to such fundamental gauges of value as earnings, dividends, book value, or cash flow. Value stocks usually are found among more economically sensitive industries such as energy, finance, or basic materials, but circumstances unique to a company in a "growth" industry also can drive its stock price down to where it represents sound fundamental value.

The Sentimental Journey

Value beats growth over the long haul because sentiment distorts what investors are willing to pay to own a stock. The aggregate holdings of a growth-style manager typically has an above-average price-earnings ratio and a below-average dividend yield. Growth portfolios also tend to be expensive relative to aggregate book value and cash flow.

Why the hefty price tag on growth stocks? In effect, growth investors pay extra because of the expectation that a company will grow its earnings rapidly. But high expectations are difficult to meet. One recent study by Josef Lakonishok, Andrei Shleifer, and Robert W. Vishny of the University of Illinois found that "Given their expectations, investors are disappointed in the performance of glamour [growth] stocks relative to out-of-favor [value] stocks."[1]

How overblown are those expectations? The study concluded that "the expected growth of glamour stocks relative to value stocks implicit in their relative multiples significantly overestimates actual future growth. . . . contrary to the market's expectations . . . glamour stocks did not grow faster than value stocks. For example, while cash flow of glamour stocks was expected to grow 11.3 percent faster, it actually grew 3 percent slower. While operating income was expected to grow 22.6 percent faster for glamour stocks, it actually grew .4 percent slower."[2] And when a company fails to match Wall Street's earnings estimates—a development known as a "negative surprise"—its stock can be hammered mercilessly.

Value stocks are priced differently. By definition, value stocks sell for below-average prices relative to their earnings or dividends. That's why they are called values. Expectations for these companies are low, and their stocks are priced to reflect their supposedly modest prospects. Not all such companies are good investments, of course, but skilled value managers can uncover overlooked gems. That's when the value investor buys. The value investor sells when the overlooked gem is no longer overlooked and the new-found attention drives its price to where it overstates the company's true potential. The value investor exploits the sentimental journey from under- to overvalued.

The value investor doesn't try to forecast *when* that transformation in sentiment will take place—that would be speculating. But the value investor knows from sound fundamental research that it *will* take place more often than not. And when it does, converts to the company's story will come looking for shares.

The Dollars and Sense of Value Investing

Seeing is believing. And what better way to appreciate what value investing can accomplish than to scrutinize the work of some of its most notable practitioners. The first record (Exhibit 1-1) is for Walter & Edwin Schloss Associates, L. P.,

E X H I B I T   1 - 1

Walter & Edwin Schloss Associates, L.P.

Year	Walter & Edwin Schloss Limited Partners Overall Gain (%) (1)	S&P 500 Total Return (%) (2)	Relative Results (%) (1) – (2)
1956	5.1	6.56	−1.46
1957	−4.7	−10.78	6.08
1958	42.1	43.36	−1.26
1959	17.5	11.96	5.54
1960	7	0.47	6.53
1961	21.6	26.89	−5.29
1962	8.3	−8.73	17.03
1963	15.1	22.8	−7.7
1964	17.1	16.48	0.62
1965	26.8	12.45	14.35
1966	0.5	−10.06	10.56
1967	25.8	23.98	1.82
1968	26.6	11.06	15.54
1969	−9.0	−8.5	−0.5
1970	−8.2	4.01	−12.21
1971	25.5	14.31	11.19
1972	11.6	18.98	−7.38
1973	−8.0	−14.66	6.66
1974	−6.2	−26.47	20.27
1975	42.7	37.2	5.5
1976	29.4	23.84	5.56
1977	25.8	−7.18	32.98
1978	36.6	6.56	30.04
1979	29.8	18.44	11.36
1980	23.3	32.42	−9.12
1981	18.35	−4.91	23.26
1982	24.1	21.41	2.69
1983	38.4	22.51	15.89
1984	6.3	6.27	0.03
1985	19.5	32.16	−12.66
1986	11.9	18.47	−6.57

Continued

EXHIBIT 1-1

Continued

Year	Walter & Edwin Schloss Limited Partners Overall Gain (%) (1)	S&P 500 Total Return (%) (2)	Relative Results (%) (1) – (2)
1987	20.2	5.23	14.97
1988	29.8	16.81	12.99
1989	2.2	31.49	−29.29
1990	−12.8	−3.17	−9.63
1991	31.1	30.4	0.7
1992	9.2	7.68	1.52
1993	20.2	9.9	10.3
1994	11.4	1.29	10.11
1995	21.2	37.53	−16.33
Annualized Return	**15.4%**	**10.8%**	**4.6%**

Sources: Walter & Edwin Schloss Associates, L.P.

a New York–based money-management firm. Over the 40-year period ended December 31, 1995, the Schloss Limited Partners earned a 15.4 percent annual compounded return versus just 10.8 percent for the S&P 500 Index.

The second track record (Exhibit 1-2) is that of Tweedy, Browne Company L. P., recognized as one of the world's foremost value-investing firms. Figures are for the equity composite of Tweedy Browne's separate accounts. Over the nearly 22-year period beginning in January 1975, the average Tweedy Browne equity account beat the overall market by 3.1 percent annually. If that doesn't sound impressive, consider that the average general equity mutual fund underperformed the S&P 500 Index by 1.96 percent per year over the 10 years ended December 31, 1996.[3]

EXHIBIT 1-2

Tweedy, Browne Company L. P.

Year	Equity Composite Tweedy, Browne Ave. Net Total Return (%) (1)	S&P 500 Total Return (%) (2)	Relative Results (%) (1) – (2)
1975	56.4	37.2	19.2
1976	40.4	23.8	16.6
1977	27.2	–7.2	34.4
1978	19.9	6.6	13.3
1979	28.7	18.7	10.0
1980	14.6	32.5	–17.9
1981	9.9	–4.9	14.8
1982	15.6	21.5	–5.9
1983	31.2	22.7	8.5
1984	15.8	6.3	9.5
1985	28.9	31.8	–2.9
1986	11.6	18.7	–7.1
1987	4.2	5.3	–1.1
1988	18.1	16.6	1.5
1989	13.2	31.7	–18.5
1990	–12.3	–3.1	–9.2
1991	24.0	30.5	–6.5
1992	14.9	7.6	7.3
1993	12.7	10.1	2.6
1994	–0.1	1.3	–1.4
1995	36.4	37.6	–1.2
1996 (9 months)	15.5	13.5	2.0
Annualized Return	**18.8%**	**15.7%**	**3.1%**

Source: Tweedy, Browne Company L.P.

Finally we come to Warren Buffett, considered by many to be America's premier investor, and a value investor all his life. Those who initially placed $10,000 into Buffett's private partnership when it opened in 1956 would have walked off in 1969, when the fund dissolved, with about $260,000.[4] (See Exhibit 1-3.)

In 1965, Buffett formed Berkshire Hathaway, a holding company designed to serve as a vehicle for the master's investments. Over the ensuing 31 years, Berkshire Hathaway outperformed the S&P 500 Index by an astounding 13.02 percent annually. (See Exhibit 1-4.)

Skill–Not Luck

Critics might argue that the extraordinary track records compiled by these value investors are the result of simple chance. But consider that in each case the performance was accomplished over many years. Exhibit 1-5 compares annualized total returns over various time periods against what investors would have earned simply by holding the "average" stock.

One valuable lesson emerges from the track records of these accomplished value practitioners: investing is a marathon, not a sprint. Our sample group showed negative returns in six percent of all years, and underperformed the market roughly one-quarter of the time (Exhibit 1-6). But the fact that superior overall results were achieved despite an occasional short-term stumble highlights the importance of taking a long-term approach to investing.

LOOK AT THE RECORD

So what? a reader might say. Weren't the superior returns noted above simply the result of the each manager's magical touch? Can the average value investor expect to do as well?

E X H I B I T   1 - 3

Buffett Partnership, Ltd.

Year	Overall Results from DJIA (%)	Partnership Results (%)	Limited Partners' Results (%)
1957	−8.4	10.4	9.3
1958	38.5	40.9	32.2
1959	20.0	25.9	20.9
1960	−6.2	22.8	18.6
1961	22.4	45.9	35.9
1962	−7.6	13.9	11.9
1963	20.6	38.7	30.5
1964	18.7	27.8	22.3
1965	14.2	47.2	36.9
1966	−15.6	20.4	16.8
1967	19.3	35.9	28.4
1968	7.7	58.8	45.6
1969	−11.6	6.8	6.6
On a cumulative or compounded basis, the results are:			
1957	−8.4	10.4	9.3
1957–58	26.9	55.6	44.5
1957–59	52.3	95.9	74.7
1957–60	42.9	140.6	107.2
1957–61	74.9	251.0	181.6
1957–62	61.6	299.8	215.1
1957–63	94.9	454.5	311.2
1957–64	131.3	608.7	402.9
1957–65	164.1	943.2	588.5
1957–66	122.9	1156.0	704.2
1957–67	165.3	1606.9	932.6
1957–68	185.7	2610.6	1403.5
1957–69	152.6	2794.9	1502.7
Annualized Rate	**7.4**	**29.5**	**23.8%**

Source: Warren E. Buffett, "The Superinvestors of Graham–and–Doddsville," *Hermes,* Fall 1984, p.7. Reprinted with permission.

E X H I B I T   1 - 4

Berkshire Hathaway Inc.

| | *Annual Percentage Change* | | |
Year	In Per–Share Book Value of Berkshire (1)	In S&P 500 with Dividends Included (2)	Relative Results (1) – (2)
1965	23.8	10.0	13.8
1966	20.3	–11.7	32.0
1967	11.0	30.9	–19.9
1968	19.0	11.0	8.0
1969	16.2	–8.4	24.6
1970	12.0	3.9	8.1
1971	16.4	14.6	1.8
1972	21.7	18.9	2.8
1973	4.7	–14.8	19.5
1974	5.5	–26.4	31.9
1975	21.9	37.2	–15.3
1976	59.3	23.6	35.7
1977	31.9	–7.4	39.3
1978	24.0	6.4	17.6
1979	35.7	18.2	17.5
1980	19.3	32.3	–13.0
1981	31.4	–5.0	36.4
1982	40.0	21.4	18.6
1983	32.3	22.4	9.9
1984	13.6	6.1	7.5
1985	48.2	31.6	16.6
1986	26.1	18.6	7.5
1987	19.5	5.1	14.4
1988	20.1	16.6	3.5
1989	44.4	31.7	12.7
1990	7.4	–3.1	10.5
1991	39.6	30.5	9.1
1992	20.3	7.6	12.7
1993	14.3	10.1	4.2
1994	13.9	1.3	12.6
1995	43.1	37.6	5.5

Notes: Data are for calendar years with these exceptions: 1965 and 1966; year ended September 30, 1967; 15 months ended December 31.
Sources: *Berkshire Hathaway Inc.,* 1995 Annual Report.

EXHIBIT 1-5

Long-Term Outperformance

Manager	Number of Years	Annual % Compound Return	Annual % Compound Return vs. Average Stock
Walter & Edwin Schloss Associates	40	15.4	+4.6
Tweedy, Browne	21.75	18.8	+3.1
Warren Buffett Partnership	13	23.8	+16.4
Berkshire Hathaway	31	23.76	+13.0

Note: Results are not strictly comparable, due to differences in the length and years being measured. The S&P 500 is used as a proxy for the average stock, except for the Warren Buffett Partnership, which uses the Dow Jones Industrial Average. Returns for the Buffett and Schloss partnerships are those of the limited partners, which are after deducting incentive fees paid to the general partner.

EXHIBIT 1-6

Short-Term Stumbles

Manager	Nominal Loss Years as % of All Years	Underperformance Years as % of All Years
Walter & Edwin Schloss Associates	15.0	27.5
Tweedy, Browne	9.1	45.9
Warren Buffett Partnership	0.0	7.6
Berkshire Hathaway	0.0	9.6

Good questions. Certainly some portfolio managers are more skilled than others. Not every investor will achieve the same results, even if they apply the same selection criteria. As in any profession, skill levels vary.

But evidence also suggests that value investors have the benefit of a superior approach to portfolio management. In other words, given the same level of expertise, the value investor wins over the long haul. The University of Illinois study noted earlier concluded that "[certain] value strategies outperform glamour strategies by 8 percent per year." The same researchers also found that "the value strategy clearly does better when the market falls. The value strategy performs most closely to the glamour strategy in the 122 positive months [of the study] other than the best 25. In the very best months, the value strategy significantly outperforms the glamour strategy and the [market] index, but not by as much as it does when the market falls sharply. Overall, the value strategy appears to do somewhat better than the glamour strategy in all [economic] states and significantly better in some states."[5]

Also, consider the following study involving all NYSE stocks by Professors Michael Berry and Mitchell Stern of the University of Virginia's Darden Graduate Business School. The study found that $10,000 invested in low P/E stocks (the bottom 20 percent of the NYSE) at the beginning of 1962 would have been worth $754,167 at the end of 1987. If you had played the *total* market route your return would have been less than one third—$229,828. (Low P/Es are an element of value investing and will be discussed more in Chapter 4.) The researchers also demonstrated that such stocks returned 16.8 percent annually compared with just 9.8 percent for S&P 500 stocks.[6]

Returns from proprietary indices compiled by the Frank Russell Company also reveal the long-term superiority of the value stocks. A $100,000 investment in the Russell 3000 Value

Index in 1979 would have grown to $1.61 million by year-end 1996, or $291,000 more than an equal-sized investment in the Russell 3000 Growth Index. (Both indices are subsets of the Russell 3000, which comprises 98 percent of the investable domestic equity universe.) Confirming data from the University of Illinois study noted earlier, the Russell 3000 Value Index outperformed its growth cousin despite significantly less volatility.

As successful as value investing has been in the U.S., evidence suggests it works even better overseas. A study of six global markets published in Financial Analysts Journal found that "value stocks outperformed growth stocks on average in each country during the period studied [January 1981 through June 1992], both absolutely and after adjustment for risk." The researchers also found that "a substantial tilt towards value stocks would have been attractive ... especially if implemented on a global basis."[7]

Does Value Still Work?

The skeptic still might be unconvinced. Hasn't the investment world changed since Walter Schloss and Warren Buffett first started looking for values in the 1950s and '60s?

Yes, financial markets have changed, but in ways that make value investing even more profitable. Two of the dominant trends of the last 30 years—the growing importance of institutional investors and the shrinking of investment time frames—each play into the hands of the patient value investor. The Lakonishok, Shleifer and Vishny study found that "Many individuals look for stocks that will earn them abnormally high returns for a few months ... Institutional money managers often have even shorter time horizons. They often cannot afford to underperform the index or their peers for any non-trivial period of time, for if they do, their sponsors will withdraw the funds. A value strategy that takes 3 to 5 years to pay off but may underperform the market in the meantime might simply be too risky for money managers from the viewpoint of career concerns."[8]

Why should the politics of money management reward value investors? "If a money manager fears getting fired before a value strategy pays off, he will avoid using such a strategy," the study concludes. "When both individuals and institution money managers prefer glamour [growth] and avoid value strategies, value stocks will be cheap and earn a higher average return."[9] In other words, the trend towards immediate financial gratification rewards the value investor by keeping a segment of stock prices cheap.

Can Cheap Stocks Be Found?

Efficient market theorists would probably answer resoundingly: "No. The market can't be beat. There are too many smart analysts that know too much about too many companies."

Well, maybe. Naturally, not every value situation turns out. But don't tell Schloss or Buffett or any other of the pros who currently take profitable advantage of specific value situations. Two cases in point: Gotaas-Larsen Shipping Corp., based in Bermuda, and Gulf & Western.

Gotaas-Larsen Shipping Corp.

Two value-investing colleagues picked up Gotaas-Larsen when it dropped from $12 to $4 a share as the result of worldwide shipping doldrums. The liquidation value of the shipper's fleet, which ranged from liquefied natural gas tankers to luxury cruise ships, was figured at $7 a share.

In 1988, Gotaas-Larsen sold its cruise business, valued at $30 million in 1982, for $275 million.[10] Barclay Brothers, British financiers, then offered $48 per share for Gotaas-Larsen.

Gulf & Western

Gulf & Western offers another value success story. At the end of 1982, G & W's book value was $28 per share. Yet, the stock was selling in the $15 range, or almost half of book value, after a year of lackluster earnings and several big write-offs had produced a net loss. The dividend yield was a respectable 4.5 percent. Therefore, G & W's stock looked like it didn't have much downside risk, but had good upside potential if the company could get its act together.

In 1984 and 1985, G & W successfully undertook one of the most extensive transformations ever done by an American company. Investors quickly realized the restructuring was successful and G & W's stock sold for over double its book value by 1987.[11]

CAN ORDINARY INVESTORS USE VALUE INVESTING?

Granted, the examples above saw professionals involved. More relevant is the question: can ordinary investors successfully apply value methods? Here the answer is a resounding yes.

The charm of value investing—its mechanical simplicity—permits investors to utilize value strategies if they are willing to be patient, to dig, and to use a modicum of common sense. Far more fun and easier, but perhaps less profitable, would be wining and dining with advisers peddling great concepts. But rewards are definitely there. In Chapter 2 and the pages to follow, methods will be presented that will help turn seeming challenges and complexities into successful value-investing rewards.

NOTES

1. Josef Lakonishok, Andrei Shleifer, Robert W. Vishny, "Contrarian Investment, Extrapolation, and Risk." University of Illinois, Urbana-Champaign. April 1993.

2. Ibid.

3. *Barron's,* January 6, 1997, p. F23.

4. John Train, *The Midas Touch* (New York: Harper & Row, 1987), p. 1.

5. Josef Lakonishok, Andrei Shleifer, Robert W. Vishny, "Contrarian Investment, Extrapolation, and Risk." University of Illinois, Urbana-Champaign. April 1993.

6. David Dreman, "The Glories of Low-P/E Investing," *Forbes,* 1987.

7. Carlo Capaul, Ian Rowley, William F. Sharpe, "International Value and Growth Stock Returns." *Financial Analysts Journal,* January-February 1993, p.27.

8. Josef Lakonishok, Andrei Shleifer, Robert W. Vishny, "Contrarian Investment, Extrapolation, and Risk." University of Illinois, Urbana-Champaign. April 1993.

9. Ibid.

10. Brett Duval Fromson, "A Low-Risk Path to Profits," *Fortune,* Fall 1988, p.14.

11. Peter D. Heerwagen, *Investing for Total Return* (Chicago: Probus, 1988), p. 52.

2 CHAPTER

Buy Straw Hats
in Winter

Here's a down-to-earth example of the difference between value and growth investing. Go to the mall on a winter day and walk through any clothing store. You'll see scores of shoppers looking at heavy coats, sweaters, and wool hats. Since these items are in season, demand—and therefore the price—will be high. Think of these shoppers as growth investors.

Meanwhile, over in a far corner of the store will be a clearance rack full of swimsuits, tank tops, and straw hats. It's winter, of course, and few people are interested in buying lightweight apparel. But every once in a while someone will walk over and buy an item for pennies on the dollar. That shopper is a value investor.

Can value investing really be as easy as buying out-of-season merchandise? And if the record of value investing clearly proves it's the road to Golconda, why isn't everyone scouring the stock pages for their own diamonds?

The reasons are not hard to find. This chapter begins with a definition of value investing and then addresses several reasons why it might not be everyone's cup of tea. The chapter also presents arguments on why an investor should "buy a business" and not "buy the stock" and why concentration on internal rather than external matters—the essence of Graham's particular time-tested value strategy—can be profitable. This chapter also presents attitudes that value investors have successfully adopted—including the "24-second" philosophy—as well as dispelling two current investing ideas that could prove harmful. Should you go against the crowd? The experts? We will discuss why thumbing your nose at the experts could be the best investment step you'll ever take. But, first things first. Let's briefly outline the value investing philosophy.

WHAT DO WE MEAN BY VALUE INVESTING?

Defining value investing can be chancy. Many investors claim to wear "value" hats. Some investors, however, have diluted the value recipe, shortened time horizons, or otherwise engaged in practices sure to make classic value investors wince.

The usual definition of value investing concentrates on identifying companies whose shares trade at cheap prices, i.e., substantially below the companies' inherent worth. (Worth, in this context, takes into account a company's longer-term average earnings together with the price for which its assets could be sold.)

Benjamin Graham outlined two methods and strategies for evaluating stocks. The first was to determine a company's earning power, a strategy that does not fall within the scope of this book.[1] His second strategy, however, does fall within the book's scope.

Under Graham's second tactic, value investors essentially ferret out companies that trade for significantly less than book or net asset value. There are other criteria; I'll go into them later.[2]

The soul of value investing is to buy company shares at a discount. The heart is simply this: At any given time there are excellent businesses that attract a good deal of attention. Meanwhile, other segments are overlooked by investors. These wallflower segments contain a wide variety of businesses in which investments could be made—if the price were right.

That is a commonplace observation. What is not so commonplace, however, is this: While many businesses are not worth what they sell for in the stock market, some businesses are almost given away. Like those straw hats in winter for the far-sighted shopper, these are the types of companies that cause a glint in the eyes of value investors. Or they should. The way to find them is by looking *internally,* that is, at the performance of the underlying business and also at its resources.

The average value investor pays no heed to *external* matters; that is, to quarterly earnings projections, market volatility, price momentum, volume, or the day-to-day prices at which a company's securities trade. Comparative analysis plays a diminished role.

LOOKING AT A VALUE STOCK: NATIONAL PRESTO

Graham cited National Presto as a typical value stock in the 1973 edition of his book, *The Intelligent Investor.* For his research on National Presto Graham used S&P statistics provided by the La Jolla, California, wire house where the author was employed. Since I was in at the beginning, I've taken the liberty of including the incident in this chapter.

At first glance, Presto was the kind of company a homemaker would love. The housewares maker invented not only the pressure cooker, but also the electric frying pan, the first steam iron that could use tap water, and the stainless steel percolator. The only thing it couldn't stir up was investor interest.

Even though the company's balance sheet was a thing of beauty, Presto's price had dipped to $21 in 1970 from a high of $45 two years earlier. At that level, it was priced at just four times earnings and 65 percent of book value. It also sold at a considerable discount from its net current assets of $27 per share. Earnings had grown from $0.77 per share in 1958 to $5.61 in 1968, when it was supplying shells for the Vietnam War. By March 1972, Presto had recovered somewhat to $34 per share, but the stock was still trading only at its enlarged net current assets and at a mere 5.5 times earnings.

Graham was not loath to put his money where his pen was. Shortly after the new edition of *The Intelligent Investor* was published, Graham purchased 1,000 shares of National Presto at $33 per share. Interestingly enough, by March 1974, I'd formed my advisory firm and purchased Presto for my clients at $28.90 per share, including commission. It was then trading at 4.5 times earnings, net current assets were $41 per share, and book value was $50. Cash items alone accounted for some $19 per share. Two years later I sold my holdings in National Presto at roughly its book value of $54.25 per share. That's a 64.3 percent gain over the two years, during a time when the overall market was losing 20.8 percent. Who says all stocks go down in a bear market?

BUYING THE BUSINESS—NOT THE STOCK

Investing in value equities should be treated like buying part ownership in a business—which, indeed, it is. In other words, it requires the same mental framework.

Like any businessman, the value investor aims to determine the company's true worth—that is, its assets and components—as well as what kind of wealth could be generated. In other words, what is the company's intrinsic value. In the case of assets, intrinsic value is what would be realized if liquidation occurred. In the case of earnings, it means the value realized by any excess returns expected compared to the returns of long-term AAA bonds.

The bottom line is simple: *Value investors first, last, and always, think of buying the business, not the stock.* These two variables—price and business value—are all that should concern a value investor.

Lack of Mystique Borders on Heretical

It's easy to see that the above strategy violates almost all current notions of "proper" investment theory. The plain truth is that some of the brightest professionals and academicians—many of whom pontificate grandly about efficient markets, dynamic hedging, betas, and alphas—might find value-investing concepts too simple. After all, there's really no mystique about it.

Admittedly, value investing requires some effort. (Nobody said it would be *that* easy.) Then too, the application of several standards means that not every horse that comes by gets ridden.

Stock traders swear by short-term quotations. Market prices may serve if an investor needs instant performance and doesn't know much about the company in which she's investing other than a handful of statistics and the latest popular story.

Investors concerned about superior long-term performance approach things differently. To them, superior long-term performance is the result of buying excellent values—and then sticking with them. As a value investor you must look for mistakes in judgment or analysis rather than short-term market prices.

GETTING RID OF TWO MYTHS

One prominent reason why many investors shy from value investing relates to two Wall Street myths that are sold over and over. The first has to do with efficient markets; the second, with betas.

Efficient Market Theory

Many academics, observers, and pundits argue that the stock market acts efficiently. That's portfolio-speak for the theory that stock prices accurately reflect everything known about a company's prospects. According to this view, studying fundamentals such as earnings and book values is as useless and unreliable as reading tarot cards or tea leaves. The reason? Undervalued stocks—or so it is claimed—don't actually exist, since security analysts have already harvested all available information and thereby ensured unfailingly appropriate prices.

Our latter-day storytellers have embellished their tales with jazzy computer printouts and a twentieth-century label—the efficient market theory, or EMT. Like Gaul, their theory is divided into three parts: weak; semi-strong; and strong.

Weak
The weak version of the efficient market theory holds that past prices have no bearing on future prices. In other words, what investors will pay to own shares of a company in the future is essentially independent of their past actions; price patterns over the long haul resemble a *random walk.*

Generally, value investors have no quarrel with the weak form. So-called technical analysis of price behavior has never served adequately as a substitute for fundamental analysis. Studies have revealed that a weak linkage between past and future prices does exist. Certainly not enough, however, to generate trading profits after transaction costs.

Semi-Strong
The semi-strong form states that markets are efficient because of the rapid and democratic way that knowledge is

dispersed in the Information Age. And yes, there is no deny-
ing that as information about companies, industries, and the
economy arrives at the marketplace, prices do instantly as-
similate the new data.

Transmitting information quickly, however, doesn't
guarantee that the conclusions drawn are accurate. Rapidly
transmitted information may suggest one picture, but a significantly different one may emerge as the ideas are inter-
preted over time.

Strong

This version of the efficient market theory holds that at any
given moment security prices already accurately reflect *all
knowable public and private information.* In other words, no
amount of skilled interpretation of available public data
would enable any investor to reach judgments that are different enough from the market price to earn greater returns.
In this view, the efforts of security analysts to identify mis-
pricings plus the knowledge of insiders are entirely successful in creating market efficiency.

The theory depends on the best of all possible worlds,
where only logical, predictable behavior is exhibited. There
is only one problem: markets simply aren't orderly or logical.
"Another practical flaw in the Rational Expectations/EMH
[efficient market hypothesis] is that not all the decisions
taken by investors are rational," writes Clifford F. Pratten of
the University of Cambridge. "Irrational influences, hope,
fear and so on, do play a part: the oft-quoted statement that
the market is driven by alternating bouts of greed and fear
sums up the position."[3]

A real-world example of opportunities created by market illogic was the author's purchase of National Value and
Manufacturing at $13.75 per share. At that price, the stock
sold for just 2.4 times earnings and two times cash flow.
The company had no debt and net current assets of $23 per
share, including $19.35 per share in cash. Therefore, cash
and cash equivalent items were purchased at 60 percent of

value, and a 42 percent earnings yield was returned on the purchase price! (The average earnings yield of the Standard & Poor's 500 over the last 50 years has been roughly 6 percent.) Obviously, the market's treatment of National Value and Manufacturing was neither efficient nor logical. Later substantial appreciation in the stock's price confirmed the market's illogic.

The best time to view the market's inherent *inefficiency* is during the main earnings reporting months of January, April, July, and October. Notice how many companies report profits that are far removed from the consensus of Wall Street analysts. If markets were truly efficient, the average (consensus) of these expectations would be close to the actual earnings. Instead, companies regularly report profits that are 10 percent, 50 percent, even 100 percent off from the consensus view.

Summary

Recent evidence calls into serious doubt many basic assumptions of the efficient market theory. According to Pratten, "The 1987 Crash, when the Dow Jones index fell by 30.7% in six days, gave a new impetus and direction to tests of the EMT and added credibility to tests which contradicted the hypothesis; because such a *large* and *swift* fall was not compatible with changes in stock market prices being determined by new information concerning fundamentals alone."[4] Pratten concludes, "Important assumptions underpinning the EMH simply do not apply in practice."[5]

Robert A. Haugen, a professor of finance at the University of California at Irvine, also has studied the EMT and found it lacking. "We now see a market that is highly inefficient and overreactive; a market literally turned upside down—where the highest-risk adjusted stocks can be expected to produce the lowest returns and the lowest-risk stocks, the highest returns!"[6]

Like Professor Pratten, Haugen found that emotions play an important role in securities pricing. "Overwhelming evidence is piling up that investors overreact to the past performance of stocks, pricing growth stocks—stocks which are expected to grow faster than average—too high and value stocks—stocks which are expected to grow slower than average—too low. Subsequent to these overreactions, growth stocks produce low returns for the investors who buy them at high prices, and similarly, value stocks produce high returns for their investors."[7]

Most value investors would certainly agree that market efficiency has increased through analytic techniques and the recognition of sound principles. But the careful study of market movements demonstrates several anomalies, including the small-company effect and the superior returns of low-P/E-ratio stocks. Those phenomena in themselves disprove efficient market theories.

In the real world—where emotions such as fear and greed abound—logic is often a scarce commodity. This situation is rewarding for the value investor, provided, however, that the gap between price and value caused by such inefficiency can be successfully exploited.

Beta Watch Out

The second Wall Street myth has cautioned investors to avoid high-beta stocks—in other words, those stocks that react extremely to market fluctuations.[8]

The beta theory, of course, has absurdly oversimplified good investment practice. This has been pointed out by many, including author John Train. Train takes the beta theory to task in *The Midas Touch,* an excellent book that provides considerable insight into the current investing philosophy of Warren Buffett.[9]

Buffett, said Train, offered the example of being able to buy $1 worth of value in the market for 75 cents. Suppose the price declined so that the same $1 worth of value could be had for 50 cents while at the same time the general market remained unchanged. Here, beta has increased but so has opportunity and safety. To reject opportunity because of an increasing beta would be absurd.

Consider Buffett's purchase of stock in The Washington Post Company roughly 24 years ago, when its market capitalization approximated just $80 million. The whole company could easily have been marketed and sold at that time for at least $400 million.

What if the company's 1973 market value had dropped even further—from $80 million to $40 million. The additional downside volatility would have made the stock's beta increase, but it also clearly would have made it a better value. Should investors have been frightened off by the higher beta? Obviously not. By 1997, The Washington Post Company had a market capitalization of $3.6 billion, up nearly 45-fold since 1973.

VALUE INVESTING: AVOIDING THE PITFALLS

Now let's examine some of the challenges ahead. Don't be alarmed: They're not that hard. You don't have to be able to play three-dimensional chess. Successful value investing rests on carefully following the precepts and directions you'll find outlined in these pages as well as establishing a particular philosophy and temperament.

Philosophical Differences

To start right out, never concern yourself with predicting future developments. In contrast to growth-stock investors, who may live and die with projections, the value investor looks only to what is indisputable and measurable right now. (Obviously certain assumption are held: What is value in the past generation will be value in time to come.)

The average value investor has better things to do than scour the financial pages for low-beta stocks or for one person's guess about the direction of interest rates or the economy. Also, pay little attention to "concept" stocks or other popular wares a registered representative might peddle. On the other hand, as we noted earlier, the value investor must view value stocks as if buying a private business. In some respects, value investors adopt the mind set of a business analyst rather than a market strategist.

First, examine a company's economic value in relation to its stock price. If you're satisfied, then appraise the people in charge—the company's management. The best way to judge managerial competence is by examining the company's published operating results. By sticking to the hard numbers, you eliminate emotional reactions that inevitably arise from a personal visit with management. Factual matters can be double-checked by a call to a company's president or chief financial officer. Failing to reach them, the investor can call the investor relations department. Don't be afraid to pick up the phone. A lot of these guys are like the Maytag repairman—lonesome. They love to talk.

No Room for Sentimentality

Here we find another cornerstone of the value approach. The value category includes every qualifying stock for which reliable data can be obtained. Every company is a potential buy. No distinction is made between "big names" and "no names," personal likes and dislikes, or well-run and poorly run companies.

Poorly run companies? Think about it for a moment. Unexpected positive things will more than likely happen to companies where management is consistently incompetent or selfish. These positive surprises can have a dramatic effect on a company's stock, especially if its price is already low. For example, a sale or liquidation of a poorly performing segment of a business could speed up the realization of substantial gains for investors.

Keep the Right Attitude

Sometimes a grim determination to sit back and do nothing is the best strategy for professional value investors to adopt. Many mistakes have been made by businessmen who are unable to sit quietly in one room and do nothing.

Patience admittedly goes against the grain. We've been trained from childhood to "do something." Time and again businessmen have built large cash positions and then lost patience. The result? Cash has been plowed into high-priced acquisitions of misunderstood businesses—only for something to do.

Mobil Oil provided an excellent example. Faced with the luxury of a large cash flow, Mobil management hustled out to acquire Montgomery Ward. The oil giant's exploration of the retail industry was a dry hole, much to management's later regrets.

No 24-Second Clock in the Investment Business

In professional basketball, either the team in possession of the ball shoots within 24 seconds or the opponent gets the ball. Shoot it or lose it. It's a different game on Wall Street. In the investment business, you can dribble and pass the ball around until you get the shot you want. No clock is ticking on the selection process. You can take as much time as necessary until just the right opportunity appears.

The value investor should clearly understand that the goal is not today's blue plate special—the hot stock of the hour, or the stock with the most momentum. In fact, value stocks at first glance are never exciting or hot. It takes time before the value of a business becomes recognized—sometimes three to five years.

The goal of the value investor is not a sudden run-up and quick cash-out, but finding an outstanding business at a sensible price, or a mediocre business at a bargain price.

Those bargain situations may happen for a variety of reasons. Perhaps the business has fallen from favor. Perhaps there's been a cyclical downturn or short-term bad news. These events, and others like them, create the buying opportunities that the skillful value investor waits patiently to exploit.

Cyclical Bad News

Take Ford as an example. In 1980 the company sustained losses amounting to $12.83 per share. Ford's red ink was caused mainly by a simultaneous economic and auto sales recession.

The result? In 1980 Ford's stock plunged to a new low of $18.50. When more losses followed over the next two years, the company was temporarily on the ropes. Ford's troubles, however, turned out to be good news for willing-to-be-patient value investors. When the economy recovered and the auto industry adapted to a changed competitive environment, Ford's stock soared. After going profitless for three years, long-term-oriented value investors could have cashed out of Ford five years later at 12 times their original investment.

Short-Term Bad News

The consequences of short-term bad news on a company's stock price can best be illustrated by the gyrations that affected two corporate icons, Union Carbide and Woolworth.

In 1984, an explosion shattered a Union Carbide chemical plant in Bhopal, India, resulting in the deaths of more than 3,800 people. In the aftermath of the tragedy, the company's stock fell sharply. Eventually, however, investors began to focus on Union Carbide's longer-term prospects, and share-holders were handsomely rewarded for their patience.

Woolworth provides another example of how short-term bad news can work to the benefit of value investors. The company overexpanded and took on too much debt during the 1980s. By 1992, Woolworth was losing nearly $500 million per year, and its stock had dropped from $36 in 1991 to just $9 in early 1996. A lost cause? Hardly. New management took over and began aggressively cutting costs, repairing the balance sheet, and adapting the company to a changed retail environment. At $9 per share, Woolworth was selling for just three times cash flow and below book value. The market was saying that the company wasn't going to survive. Eventually, however, investors recognized that their emotion-based re-action had been overdone. Woolworth stock closed 1996 at $22 per share, a 135 percent gain in less than a year.

Going Against the Crowd

Value investing has usually meant going against conven-tional wisdom. The average value investor will find it ex-tremely profitable to simply ignore investment world chatter about what the market did and where it's going.

Far more profitable is to have the courage of your own convictions. Whether the crowd agrees or disagrees is unim-portant. The plain truth is that most people will miss the point of a value investor's decision.

For example, in the months prior to the 1987 stock-mar-ket crash, many true Graham-and-Dodders were unable to find enough stocks to buy at reasonable prices. Rather than overpay, they chose instead to hold Treasury bills. Retreating to cash during a raging bull market took courage, but it turned out to be the right decision when stock prices fell by 21 percent on October 19, 1987.

Obviously, crowd-bucking is easier said than done. Most people follow the crowd, content to buy when others buy and to sell when others sell.

Going Against the Experts

Value investors frequently butt heads with so-called experts. That's all right; it's not dangerous. The use of experts to pontificate and predict has a long tradition. Commissions of experts have had an enviable record of telling us what happened and why, but a lamentable score when they proceed from there to tell us what will happen next.

In 1486, King Ferdinand and Queen Isabella set up an expert committee headed by the bishop of Ávila, Hernando de Talavera, to study Columbus's plan for reaching the Indies by sailing west. After four years' work, the committee reported that such a voyage was impossible because: (1) the Western Ocean was infinite and unnavigable; (2) if Columbus reached the Antipodes he could not get back; and (3) there were no Antipodes because the greater part of the globe was covered with water, as St. Augustine had said earlier. Fortunately, Columbus did not listen to the experts.[10]

Many people still give blanket acceptance to whatever market pundits say or write. Their viewpoints are often persuasive enough to compel investors to act without first thinking the situation through. Unfortunately, as the following data indicate, the jump-first-and-ask-questions-later approach can be hazardous to your financial health.

Experts Frequently Wrong

Each day we are bombarded by opinions about what the market is going to do next. A week's worth of listening and/or viewing provides the average investor with the information that a bull market is becoming "long in the tooth," or that stock prices are "overextended," or that the market is "climbing a wall of worry." The precise implication and meaning of these phrases is left to the imagination. The same market activity is reported from differing slants, then warmed up and rehashed for the evening news.

Would you profit by this counsel? Look at Exhibit 2-1, which was compiled from recommendations made by market forecasters between 1963 and 1996. The weekly publication *Investors Intelligence* monitors sentiment figures from leading advisory services. The data indicate that even investment professionals are consistently wrong about the short-term direction of the market.

For example, only 15 percent of advisors were bearish in the days before the market began a nearly 50 percent decline in January 1973. By the time stock prices finally bottomed in late 1974, 60 percent of advisors had turned bearish. In other words, they were 600 days late and several billions of dollars short. In August 1982, as stocks were about to embark on a spectacular bull market, only 39 percent of advisors were bullish. Yet just prior to the market crash in October 1987, only about a quarter of advisors thought a bear market was at hand.

The bottom line is that no one has a crystal ball, not even the so-called experts. Acting on the basis of someone's projection is likely to result in your buying at market tops and selling out near the bottom.

The Price of Following the Crowd

Moving with current "newspaper darlings" has always cost dearly. Yet many investors overlook the fact that the simple law of averages dictates that some darlings will have good short-term records, and this subjugates vital critical thinking. Even a stopped clock is right twice a day.

Please understand that I am not suggesting that good advice isn't available, or that in all cases you should ignore it. Simply be careful to apply critical judgment to each conclusion and recommendation. Following are three questions to ask yourself before taking someone's advice and diving into a new stock position:

E X H I B I T 2 - 1

Advisory Sentiment at Market Turns

Date	Bulls (%)	Bears (%)	Correction (%)	Change in S&P 500 Index Over Subsequent Cycle (%)
February 9, 1966	34.9	11.9	53.2	–22.2
October 7, 1966	25.4	52.5	22.1	+48.1
November 28, 1968	40.9	27.3	31.8	–36.1
May 26, 1970	29.0	56.5	14.5	+73.5
January 11, 1973	61.1	15.3	23.6	–48.2
October 3, 1974	40.0	60.0	0.0	+73.1
September 21, 1976	60.3	11.8	27.9	–19.4
March 6, 1978	35.5	61.8	2.7	+61.7
November 28, 1980	34.8	37.1	28.1	–27.1
August 12, 1982	39.0	41.0	20.0	+228.8
August 25, 1987	59.8	17.2	23.0	–33.5
December 4, 1987	28.0	45.8	26.2	+64.8
July 16, 1990	45.2	34.7	20.1	–20.0
October 11, 1990	41.4	50.0	8.6	+150.0 *

*Through December 31, 1996.
Source: *Investors Intelligence.*

1. Does the recommendation seem logical?
2. Can you think of factors that may have been left out?
3. Is what you're getting plain-vanilla wisdom or a look behind the obvious?

Keep in mind that following the crowd can trap professional investors as well as novices. In fact, it helped me blow a decision concerning Union Carbide.

My firm had originally purchased Union Carbide in November 1981 at $48.50 per share. (For the sake of discussion the figures have been left unadjusted for splits.) Based on value criteria, the purchase made sense. Union Carbide traded at five times earnings, 66 percent of book value, with a dividend yield of 6.5 percent. The company's debt load was reasonable. Somewhat smugly, I watched for three years while the stock appreciated.

Then came Bhopal. The public was inundated with scare headlines: Union Carbide would lose billions. Since the national debt seemed smaller than the apparent loss, I sold Union Carbide in December 1984 at $34.125. To be perfectly fair, client pressures and tax considerations also had played a role. However, the wheel turned and things settled down. It became apparent that Union Carbide's losses would be much less than once anticipated.

Since then, Union Carbide's stock has risen substantially—at one time topping $98 per share when a takeover threat occurred. Consequently, selling Union Carbide at a little over $34 proved to be a poor decision.

CONCLUSION

Keep in mind that although the market knows what happened in the past, it cannot predict the future. Surprises are what make the market move.

Certainly, some elements can be estimated. We can assume that what has generally been true of business conditions in the past will continue to be true. Gross domestic product growth has averaged around 3 percent annually for 200 years, and chances are it won't vary greatly in the foreseeable future. Profit margins have remained the same for the last 50 years. Usually the nature of a business does not dramatically change, although no one knows how quickly the company's fortunes may shift or how well a new product will sell.

In Chapter 3 I'll show you how to search for specific businesses to own and how to go about forming your value universe.

NOTES

1. Graham & Dodd, *Security Analysis* (New York: McGraw-Hill, 1934), p. 405.
2. Benjamin Graham, *The Intelligent Investor* (New York: Harper & Row, 1947), p. 53.
3. Cliff Pratten, *The Stock Market* (Cambridge: University Press, 1993), p. 174.
4. Ibid., p. 25.
5. Ibid., p. 175.
6. Robert A. Haugen, *The New Finance: The Case Against Efficient Markets* (Englewood Cliffs, NJ: Prentice Hall, 1995), p. 1.
7. Ibid.
8. Beta-coefficient theories propose that securities prices are constantly and correctly assessing trade-offs between risk and reward. Low-quality securities appreciate and decline more than do high-quality securities. Beta itself is defined as a security's estimated market sensitivity. That sensitivity is measured in terms of an expected incremental percentage return associated with a 1 percent change in return of an index like the Standard & Poor's 500.
9. John Train, *The Midas Touch* (New York: Harper & Row, 1987), p. 55.
10. Walter Wriston, *Risk & Other Four-Letter Words* (New York: Harper & Row, 1986), p. 54.

PART TWO

HOW TO FIND
VALUE COMPANIES

3 CHAPTER

The Search for Value

So you've decided to become a value investor. What securities should you buy? *The Wall Street Journal*, the Rosetta stone of American finance, provides no clues. Open its stock-listing pages and a sea of companies swim before you in agate-sized type. There is little to distinguish one company from another. So how does the value investor create a portfolio of value stocks?

Building a value portfolio is actually not difficult. For the most part, only a few simple and logical procedures are involved. It's somewhat akin to buying a house. Chances are that when you shop for a house you're most interested in location and you screen out those that are unsuitable for one reason or another. In certain respects, that's how we build a list of potential value stocks. We do it by screening.

The present chapter addresses the screening process and starts you on your way. Given that know-how, the average value investor can quickly assemble a universe of potential value-stock candidates.

Don't worry if, at the beginning, the universe seems overly abundant. In the next three chapters you'll find practical tips and clues on how to whittle down the list to something manageable. You'll also be directed to spots where investment opportunities can be found that offer the potential for hefty profits with adequate safety. How does a value investor build a solid portfolio? Where can the data necessary to evaluate value stocks be found? When should value stocks be sold? Answers to these questions are crucial to investment success.

VALUE BASICS

First, let's do some preliminary housekeeping. Following are answers to four fundamental questions regarding value investing.

What Are Value Stocks?

Value stocks are corporate shares that sell for less than the company's intrinsic worth. How much less depends on the situation, but a rule of thumb that most successful value investors follow is about one-third less.

Does It Matter Where the Company Is Headquartered?

Location or trading area is immaterial. Value companies are found in San Diego, Fargo, London, and Sri Lanka. They could be listed on the NYSE or the Amex, or traded over-the-counter. Excellent bargain stocks have been found buried among the koalas in Sydney, Australia, or mixed among the Volkswagens in Frankfurt, Germany.

Does It Matter in What Industry or Business the Company Operates?

The amount of sales or type of industry are irrelevant. Sales of value companies range from $5 million to $80 billion, and the companies come from a variety of industries. (The average value investor pays scant attention to the copious lists of companies by sales, etc., published by *Fortune, Forbes,* and similar magazines.)

What Types of Companies Should Be Avoided?

This point rests more with psychological and analytical aspects, but is exceptionally important: *Invest only in what you understand.* Knowledge provides an important measure of self-defense. Understanding a business means that you won't give way to scare headlines that could influence your investment decisions over the short term. Also, understanding a business might act as a spur to facilitate the digging necessary to uncover important information.

PUTTING TOGETHER A UNIVERSE

Identifying possible value investments sounds, and is, simple enough. Before starting, however, the value investor would find it prudent to broadly sieve out businesses to own from ones to avoid. Following are a few ideas on how to spot a business worth owning.

1. Look for a high return on invested capital over a period of years. That's always a good sign. The long-term average for businesses has been 12 percent to 13 percent annually on beginning capital.

2. Get a feeling for management, either in person or from published material like annual reports. Look for management that not only thinks like an owner but has staked out its own corporate share. That's an important clue. If a president owns 20 percent or more of the outstanding stock, then we both want the same thing—an increased share price. Managers tied only by salary and benefits aren't rowing the same boat as shareholders.

3. Search for businesses that create profits in the form of real cash, not just phony earnings

generated by the magic wand of accounting. Creative accounting can make profits look healthier than they really are.

This brings to mind an illuminating story told by Abraham J. Briloff, a distinguished author and professor of accounting. The tale concerns an underwriter who, charged with finding an auditor, called in partners from several major accounting firms. Each partner was interviewed and asked, "What does two plus two equal?" Each of the respondents replied, "Four, of course"each, that is, but the one selected. His answer, after some serious reflection, was, "What number did you have in mind?"

4. Check inventory turnover. Is it rapid compared with its industry? Is there a high return on the total of plant plus inventory? Are earnings predictable?

5. Glance over the company's business. Good businesses generally have clearly defined products or services.

6. Look for managers who talk in terms of return to shareholders and controlling expenses rather than sales growth.

The Noland Company, a Virginia-based distributor of electrical and plumbing supplies, serves as a case in point. Its return-on-assets and return to the shareholder over the years have been sub par. The company had continually communicated to shareholders in a manner that emphasized sales growth above all else. No mention was made that the sales growth did not directly contribute to growing the shareholders' bottom line.

Yet here's an important point about the single overriding principle of value investing: getting the right price. In spite of the Noland Company's preoccupation with sales growth at the expense of earnings, the author purchased shares of the company when they traded below net-net current assets per share and far below the market value of all assets. And it turned out to be a satisfactory investment, mainly due to the low price paid.

How to Spot Businesses to Avoid

How can an investor spot undesirable businesses? That's no problem either. In most instances, simply reverse the above characteristics.

1. Duck businesses loaded with debt. Mushrooming debt frequently indicates that things are going wrong. If that's the case, the company could eventually collapse or need to refinance its debt on unfavorable terms. Here's a good rule of thumb: *Businesses should have no more debt than equity.* Of course, that's not true in all cases. The rule doesn't apply to financial companies, which live on the spread between borrowed money (deposits) and lending rates. Of all the aspects of investing, however, this is the area in which you can best control your risk. Certainly you can't control what happens to the economy or the overall market. And you can't control business risk, i.e., outside circumstances that might adversely impact a specific company. But you can control financial risk by making sure that you're buying only those companies that haven't mortgaged their own futures by taking on more debt than they can handle. Before buying a company, give it a thorough financial health checkup.

2. Run from corporate managers who are more concerned with perquisites, golden parachutes, bonuses, and excessively high salaries in relation to the return to shareholders. How does the value investor get answers to these concerns? Simply thumb through a company's SEC-required filings, such as the 10-K report or notice of shareholders' meeting and proxy statement. Also take a quick glance at industry reports, which provide the going rates for top executives within that industry.

3. Don't invest in businesses that generate money through accounting legerdemain rather than real cash. Such businesses require more investment as sales grow, resulting in a lack of working capital. Look at cash-flow figures; a healthy cash flow indicates that a company can pay all of its bills with enough left over to buy shares, pay out a larger dividend, or invest.

4. Detour around companies that change character every time a hot idea appears on the horizon. Many defense contractors, for example, promote sweeping and risky new programs just to stay in business. Other managers assume so much risk it is literally a "bet your company" circumstance.

5. Stay away from companies committed to providing services or commodities at fixed prices for a long time in the future. Inflationary rises could wreak havoc here.

6. Bypass capital-intensive companies. Often the cash flow of such companies is insufficient to provide a satisfactory return while still maintaining plant at competitive levels. These companies must regularly borrow or issue stock to stay even.

7. Be particularly cautious about businesses subject to government regulation. These firms generally don't make good long-term investments, since their rates of return are limited by law.

8. Watch out for companies with different classes of stock. Shareholders may be disenfranchised through limited or nonvoting stock. Also be careful to avoid foreign companies issuing different classes of stock for nondomestic shareholders. These shares may trade at substantially different levels from those of stocks owned by domestic investors.

9. Set aside companies with managements that only occasionally initiate cost-reduction programs. Cost reduction should be an ongoing way of doing business.

10. Avoid companies that continually issue additional shares. Each secondary equity offering dilutes the ownership value of existing shareholders. The dilution also lowers a company's earnings per share, an important factor in determining a stock's market value. Be especially cautious if the proceeds from a secondary stock offering are used to invest in businesses with lower rates of return, or those for which management seems ill prepared. Remember, a bigger pie is not always a better pie.

Areas to Examine

Now that you've learned the general principles that guide a value investor, let's examine a few specific areas where opportunities for investment might be found.

• **Out of Favor Industries.** Look at companies or sectors relegated to the scrap heap by the public. You won't need to search very hard; at any moment one industry or another usually has fallen on hard times. For example, stresses on the financial system in the aftermath of the 1990–91 recession resulted in tremendous bargains in the banking sector. Many banks sold for below book value. As the economy recovered, regional and money-center banks staged a powerful rally.

• **Geographic Hard Times.** Also be on the lookout for troubles unique to a particular geographic region. In the 1980s, the collapse of energy prices temporarily depressed economies in the oil patch of Texas and Oklahoma. Budget cuts in the defense sector hurt the California economy in the early 1990s. Remember that you're looking to profit from the investing public's overly emotional reaction to a temporary situation.

• **New Lows.** Another source of potential bargains is the daily stock tables, where you'll find information on companies making new lows. Major business publications like *Investors Business Daily* or *The Wall Street Journal* regularly list companies that made new 12-month lows the previous day. In most cases, however, it's prudent to avoid glamour stocks, since everyone knows about them. A much better bet are companies that are registering one-half of a previous 12-month high. Such stocks could warrant further investigation.

• **Value Portfolios.** You also might study the portfolios of value investors who have put together lengthy and outstanding track records. For example, examine the equity offerings of value-based fund groups such as Templeton or Mutual Shares to see if their stock holdings meet your criteria. Simply write for a fund's shareholder report, which lists its holdings as of the most recent semiannual period. [**Warning:** Don't buy an issue just because some outstanding investor has done so. You must understand and have confidence in the logic of the purchase to avoid selling at the wrong time or for the wrong reason.]

• **Media.** Good value-based ideas can be found in such publications as *Barron's*, *The Wall Street Journal*, *The New York Times*, *Investors Business Daily*, or *The Financial Times*. These publications each print rosy developments—and some not so rosy—about companies that Wall Street already loves. Occasionally, however, you'll also discover information about companies that meet value criteria such as having undervalued assets.

• **IPOs.** Initial public offerings (IPOs) are not recommended for the average value investor. The hype that usually accompanies an IPO usually pushes its valuation beyond the range that would interest a value investor. Price-earnings ratios for IPOs, for example, can reach double or triple that of the overall market; some of the hotter new offerings sell on nothing more than a wing and a prayer. With expectations set so high, the odds of disappointment are too great. A value approach to stock selection requires that investors pay only for what is seen, not for what is only hoped.

Young public companies shouldn't be dismissed out of hand, however. There is a time to look at them, but in most cases it's after the stock has traded for a period and the initial fanfare has faded. Problems may have arisen in the young company's fortunes: Either management can't handle growth, fails at diversification, and expands too rapidly; or competition becomes more intense.

Two scenarios typically might occur: The stock is richly priced in the offering, rises for a while, then falls back as earnings difficulties arise. Or, the company's stock is overpriced to begin with and immediately falls below the initial offering price.

Bargains are there for the asking in the IPO market if you have the patience to look and wait. You should determine, however, whether any problems with a young company are only temporary and will be rectified in a reasonable time.

• **New Issue Closed-End Funds.** The same advice applies to newly issued closed-end funds. The prudent value investor will avoid them. Purchasing such funds at an initial offering price doesn't make good value sense.

Closed-end funds are a type of mutual fund whose number of shares outstanding is fixed at the time of the initial public offering. Investors wanting to buy or sell shares of a closed-end fund after the offering must exchange shares among themselves—like trading in IBM or Microsoft stock—rather than through the fund. Closed-end funds trade on exchanges such as the NYSE at whatever price buyers and sellers agree upon.

Suppose an investor takes a flyer on a new closed-end fund at the offering for $12 per share. Chances are good that a 7.5 percent commission has been tacked on to the purchase price. Right away the net asset value of the fund has dropped to $11.14 per share. If the fund is discounted from net asset value—a common occurrence—the investor is really pushed behind the eight ball.

• **Arbitrage.** Value investors have long been interested in arbitrage situations. Indeed, Benjamin Graham makes a special point of arbitrage in his writings. However, during the past five years the arbitrage community has grown larger, mainly because of the wide assortment of takeover bids that have come down the pike.

Arbitrage issues usually trade 1 to 5 percent below a proposed takeover price, reflecting uncertainties over the deal—and the wait for the payoff. Arbitrageurs buy with the idea of selling to the takeover company and hope to make 5 percent on capital invested for only a few months.

Arbitrage is fairly speculative and certainly not an "investment" in the traditional sense. Occasionally, however, value investors can find opportunities in arbitrage that provide an appropriate margin of safety.

How do you take advantage of acceptable arbitrage situations? Scout for large discounts from takeover prices in situations with the following characteristics: (1) friendly offers; (2) financing easy to accomplish; (3) reasonable takeover prices compared to the worth of the business (thus limiting your downside in the case of noncompletion); (4) expected annualized rate of return at a minimum of 25 to 30 percent; and (5) generally smaller, lesser-known buyouts, which avoid the competition from risk arbitrage firms and others.

Arbitrage is risky. The prudent course is to avoid making an arbitrage-based investment until after you've done your homework using the guidelines noted above.

SOURCES OF FINANCIAL INFORMATION

Now that you know what to look for in a value stock, the next step is to find out where to look. Informational sources generally fall into two broad categories: print and electronic, i.e., the Internet. Following are listings of some of the best sources from these groups.

Print

The Wall Street Journal
200 Liberty Street
New York, NY 10281
(800) 568-7625
Daily newspaper; national and international news, prices.

Investors Business Daily
12655 Beatrice Street
Los Angeles, CA 90066
(800) 306-9744
Daily newspaper; emphasis on financial-market information.

The New York Times
229 West 43rd Street
New York, NY 10036-3959
(800) 631-2500
Daily newspaper; national and international news, analysis, prices.

Barron's
200 Liberty Street
New York, NY 10281
(800) 544-0422
Weekly newspaper; summaries, analysis, interviews, prices.

Value Line Investment Survey
711 Third Avenue
New York, NY 10017
(800) 833-0046
One-page reports and analysis for 1,700 companies; industries updated weekly; all reports updated once every 13 weeks.

Morgan Stanley Capital International Perspective
Morgan Stanley, Inc.
1633 Broadway
New York, NY 10019
(212) 703-4000
Price and financial data on 1,750 companies.

The Financial Times
14 East 60th Street
New York, NY 10126
(212) 319-0704
Daily newspaper; international news and prices.

Electronic

Compustat
http://www.CompuStat.com/
Database of over 9,500 active and 8,000 inactive
companies; Screening capability.

Bloomberg
http://www.Bloomberg.com/bbn/index.html
Financial news, information, columns; corporate
profiles.

Hoover's Company Capsules
http://207.13.58.34/cgi-bin/show_file.cgi?sno-2393688
&file=/CD_home.htmlx
Information on more than 10,000 domestic and
international corporations; links to SEC filings, news
searches.

CONCLUSION

Chapter 3 has presented general guidelines for picking companies based on a value approach. The screening process was
also addressed, as well as several key places to look for
bargain issues. More filtering remains to be done, so the next
three chapters will present additional guidelines and tips for
making your selections.

4

CHAPTER

The Filtering Process

Several methods were presented in Chapter 3 that allow value investors to distinguish between "good" and "bad" companies. That's a good start, but further refinement is still necessary. For example, even some "good" companies might be too risky for most investors.

This chapter will present guidelines that can be used as tools to analyze and eliminate "too-risky" companies. Also included are five tests that value investors can use to determine an investment's intrinsic value and its margin of safety. Screening shortcuts that stick closely to Benjamin Graham's beliefs are also presented.

Let's begin the filtering process by screening for risk. Eliminate a company if any of the following criteria applies:

1. Losses were sustained within the past five years.
2. Total debt is greater than 100 percent of total tangible equity.
3. Share price is above book value.

4. Earnings yield is less than twice current long-term (20-year) AAA bond yields. [A company's earnings yield is its price earnings ratio turned inside out. For example, if a stock is selling for $30 per share with earnings of $2 per share, its price-earnings (P/E) ratio is 15 ($30 / $2 = 15). To get the earnings yield, divide the P/E ratio by 1.0. In this case, the earnings yield would be 6.6% (1 / 15 = 0.066, or 6.6%)].

Admittedly, these guidelines are strict. Is there room for exceptions? Yes, but be careful not to rationalize yourself into taking on too much risk. The *experienced* value investor might possibly ignore one or more of the criteria, but only if compelling and well-researched reasons exist for doing so. For example, the second criterion might be overlooked if a company's debt has a low interest rate, or if a company's earnings are especially strong and stable. Or, number three could be ignored, provided the company has sustained high rates of return on book value. If that analysis proves too tricky, however, it may be safer to follow the precise guidelines.

FIVE TESTS FOR VALUE

Eliminating high-risk companies will shrink the value list some; filtering for value will reduce it even more.

Graham listed five tests for value and five for safety. He did so not for professors and academicians, but to rescue average investors who had become swamped by Wall Street's blather.

Stocks were true bargains, he believed, if they met only one of the value criteria listed below plus only one of the safety criteria.

The five tests for value are:

1. The earnings yield should be at least twice the AAA bond yield. (The careful reader will note

we've already eliminated companies not meeting this criterion.)

2. The stock's price/earnings ratio should fall among the lowest 10 percent of the equity universe.
3. The stock's dividend yield should be at least two-thirds of the long-term AAA bond yield.
4. The stock's price should be no more than two-thirds of the company's tangible book value per share.
5. The company should be selling in the market for no more than two-thirds of its net current assets.

The five tests for safety are as follows:

1. A company should owe no more than it's worth, i.e., total debt should not exceed book value. (In accounting terms, the company's debt/equity ratio should be less than 1.0.)
2. Current assets should be at least twice current liabilities.
3. Total debt should be less than twice net current assets.
4. Earnings growth should have been at least 7 percent per annum compounded over the previous decade.
5. As an indication of earnings stability, there should have been no more than two annual earnings declines of 5 percent or more during the previous decade.

MARGIN OF SAFETY

One common theme that recurs throughout Graham's work is the importance of creating a margin of safety. Although the future is unpredictable, we do know that nearly every business eventually encounters the proverbial rainy day.

When stormy weather hits, the value investor wants protection.

Purchasing a stock at a low enough price provides a certain degree of protection, even if a company later has problems. That's because a company's assets or long-term earning power remains far above the firm's actual market valuation.

For example, let's say investors bought stock in Company A at 50 percent of fair value and afterwards Company A fell on hard times. Since the investors' purchase price was so low, they still might come out with at least their initial investment, even though Company A's value subsequently dropped.

But suppose that Company B's stock was purchased at 40 times earnings and five times book value per share. At those valuation levels, any amount of bad news about the company would make it difficult or impossible for investors to recoup their losses over any reasonable period.

Building in a margin of safety through a favorable purchase price provides an important hedge that takes miscalculations—or bad luck—into account. Think of it like going to the beach for a picnic. Before you put down your basket, you check to see how far the waves are running onto the shore. But you don't just settle on a spot six inches back from the waterline—that's too close for comfort. You put your basket down well away from the waterline. That added distance is your margin of safety for those few times when you know Mother Nature will act out of the ordinary.

Shortcuts Speed Things Up

Human beings are constantly striving to find shortcuts. It doesn't matter whether it's a new route for driving to the store, or a faster procedure for doing your taxes, ways are constantly being devised to do it quicker and better.

That same principle holds true in value investing. The prudent investor could benefit from two shortcuts; both save considerable time and energy. The first deals with price-earnings (P/E) multiples. The second shortcut takes into account a company's net-net value.

Track P/E Multiples

Tracking P/E ratios works superbly, at least for a quick initial screen. Simply scour any of the sources listed in Chapter 3 to find companies whose P/E multiple is less than half that of the overall market.

Remember from our earlier tests for safety that a company's price-earnings ratio, or P/E, is the relationship between its stock price and its earnings. A company selling for $40 per share with $2 per share of earnings would have a P/E ratio of 20 ($40 / $2 = 20).

Next, determine the P/E ratio of the S&P 500 Index. In this case, we're using the popular benchmark as a proxy for the entire U.S. equities market. Again, most of the financial sources listed in Chapter 3 provide this information.

For purposes of our example, let's suppose the P/E of the S&P 500 is 14, which also happens to be its long-term average. In that case, you would hunt for companies selling at less than seven times earnings.

Any stock that meets that criterion qualifies as a potential bargain. The more a company earns relative to its stock price, the lower its P/E. It follows then, that the lower a company's P/E relative to the overall market, the better the bargain. Comparing P/E ratios of similar stocks also helps determine the best buy.

(Over the last 50 years, the P/E ratio of the S&P 500 has ranged from a low of roughly 8 times earnings to a high of about 24 times earnings. Inflation is the primary factor influencing the market's overall valuation. When inflation is high, interest rates also tend to be high. That, in turn, makes yields on competing asset classes such as bonds and cash equivalents more attractive, diverting money away from stocks and depressing valuations. When inflation soared to 13 percent in 1974, for example, the market's P/E ratio fell to just eight times earnings. Conversely, low or falling inflation pushes cash and bond yields lower, usually leading to elevated equity-market multiples.)

The Net-Net Method

Graham's most famous theory was that investors should buy stocks at prices of no more than two-thirds of the company's current assets (cash and equivalents on hand, including immediately salable inventory), minus all liabilities (including off-balance-sheet liabilities such as capital leases or unfunded pension liabilities). Nothing was paid for permanent assets such as property, plant, and equipment, or intangible assets such as goodwill.

Graham held that if a company traded at two-thirds of this amount—known as net-net current assets—*and was profitable*, then investors needed no other yardstick.

"What about companies that qualified except for current losses?" I asked Graham. Those companies, he believed, were dangerously situated. Losses constantly burn up corporate assets and could incinerate the appropriate margin of safety.

Today, elevated valuations in the United States equity market make it nearly impossible to find a profitable company selling at a one-third discount to its net-net current assets. However, using the databases listed in Chapter 3, value investors can screen for those companies with the lowest net-net asset ratios.

GRAHAM'S SECOND BEST-KNOWN METHOD

Graham's other dictum, slightly more complicated, involved three linked parts: earnings yield, dividend yield, and balance sheet debt.

Earnings Yield

Bargain stocks, he believed, required earnings yields of more than twice the yield on AAA long-term bonds. (Yield is just another way of saying "rate of return on your investment.")

You'll remember from our earlier example that a company's earnings yield is its price-earnings ratio expressed as a percentage of its stock price. To find a company's earnings yield, simply divide 1 by its P/E. If Company A sells for 10 times earnings, it would have an earnings yield of 10 percent (1 / 10 = 0.10, or 10 percent).

[**Caution:** Don't confuse earnings yield with dividend yield. Both types of yields are expressed as a percentage of the market price, but the dividend yield is the amount actually paid shareholders.]

Now suppose AAA bonds yield 8 percent. Under those circumstances, a bargain stock would be one with an earnings yield of 16 percent or better. (An earnings yield of 16 corresponds to a P/E ratio of 6.25.)

Or suppose AAA bonds currently yield 7 percent. Then, for the stock to be an appropriate value stock, the earnings yield would need to be 14 percent—the same as seven times earnings.

Dividend Yield

Dividend yield was the next segment of Graham's three-part criteria. Dividend yields, he said, must be no less than two-thirds of the current AAA bond yield. In other words, when long-term AAA bonds yield 9 percent, the value investor looks for stocks with dividend yields of no less than 6 percent.

Balance Sheet Debt

Balance sheet debt was Graham's final leg. His general rule regarding debt was that companies should owe no more than they are worth.

Graham reasoned that debt was a major negative factor because it created heavy interest expense that could easily drain a company's assets. Investing in debt-burdened companies means gambling that future earnings will be high enough to meet debt service. Better to scout out companies with small debts.

How Small Is a Small Debt Load?

How small is small? Look for debt payments that are no more than one-third of a company's earnings *at their cyclical low.* That's a good rule of thumb, although it isn't hard and fast. What might be considered a healthy debt ratio depends on the nature of the company and its business.

For example, equipment leasing companies live and die by debt financing. Chances are good that such companies will carry more debt than oil exploration and development firms. Financial companies such as banks use borrowed funds that, in the main, originate from customers' savings and checking accounts. Their profit comes from the spread—the difference between the cost of the borrowed money and what can be achieved with it. Solidly financed banks may have only 6 percent of total assets in equity and the rest mainly borrowed. Surprisingly, that could be considered a safe balance sheet. In general, utilities pile up more obligations than industrial companies, since they're guaranteed a certain return.

Now let's begin the *really* fine tuning. The focus will be narrowed still more in Chapter 5.

5

CHAPTER

Narrowing Your Focus

Now the real work begins: the pragmatic, hard-headed, and often cold-hearted analysis of a company.

Begin your analysis by reminding yourself of the overriding question of value investing: Would you want to own this business? To answer that question, of course, you need facts. Lots of facts, including all available information about a company's history, its type of business, and its potential for cyclical highs and lows. Compiling this laundry list of data may seem boring, but if used correctly, these cold, hard facts make the difference between a successful investment and one that goes bust.

It has been said that value investors resemble detectives, and there is a good deal of merit in that observation. Value investors obtain all possible information on a company, but don't take anything at face value.

This chapter explains where to locate and track the corporate "paper trail." Included are tips and clues regarding what the investor should look for, as well as where to be cautious. At first, much of the reading material might seem like hopeless and arcane jargon. But don't be discouraged. Like anything else, the necessary insight will develop after you read a few of the documents.

DIG! DIG! DIG!

Consider Jim Kennedy, a young securities analyst for T. Rowe Price, who once traveled to the gold fields of South Africa to seek first-hand information about precious-metals stocks.

In South Africa, Kennedy journeyed two miles underground to explore one of the world's deepest mines. Next, Kennedy's quest for information took him to extreme northern Canada, where a new generation of gold-mining companies had emerged.

It isn't necessary for the average value investor to travel to the far corners of the earth to understand a company. But the investor does need to scan financial and narrative material prepared by companies along SEC guidelines. Chances are good that you'll uncover some real gems.

FOOD FOR THOUGHT—AND INVESTING

Following are documents that should receive special attention:

- **Form 10-K** is the official *annual* business and financial report most companies must file with the SEC.
- **Form 10-Q** is the *quarterly* financial report. Included are material and extraordinary events that occurred during the reported three-month period.
- **Form 8-K** is a report filed with the SEC within *15 days* of any unscheduled material event or corporate change.

- **Annual reports** are the most important way many public corporations communicate directly with their shareholders.
- **Quarterly reports** are statements that many companies mail directly to their shareholders.
- **Notice of annual meeting and proxy statements** are mailed to shareholders to solicit votes for the election of directors and to disclose such matters as officer salaries and insider stock holdings. Companies not soliciting proxies disclose such information in Part II of Form 10-K.
- **Merger proxy statements** are issued when shareholders are to vote on an asset-conversion matter such as a merger, acquisition, or consolidation sale of assets. When new securities are to be issued, the merger proxy statement can serve as a prospectus and as an S-4 Registration.
- **Prospectuses** are part of registration statements and are issued when securities are to be offered publicly. The principal registration forms are the S-1 (a generalized form) and the S-7, a short form used by companies with relatively healthy operating histories.
- **Cash tender offering circulars** are made available to shareholders when a publicly announced offer is made to buy shares for cash from a general list of shareholders.

TWO REASONS MATERIAL IS USEFUL

Once the information has been gathered, how useful is it? How limited? In contrast to "smart-money" traders, value investors would find such data useful for at least two reasons.

First, the information is straightforward and trustworthy. There aren't many liars to be found among those responsible for preparing these documents, if only because few lawyers, accountants, or investment bankers are going to jeopardize their livelihoods and / or reputations for the benefit of management and large shareholders. (That isn't to say the documents are wholly complete and accurate. Most of the shortcutting tends to involve relative judgments as to what is material and hence should be disclosed.)

Second, document preparation follows well-established rules regarding format and antifraud provisions. Federal securities law makes it illegal, in connection with the purchase or sale of any security, for any person, directly or indirectly "to make any untrue statement of a material fact or to omit to state a material fact."

Naturally, all documents aren't perfect. And these documents will not disclose everything the investor needs to know. But the corporate paper trail provides an excellent way to avoid securities that would be unattractive at *any price.*

Pay particularly close attention to the auditors' letter, found at the end of the audited financial statement. Such letters can be "clean," i.e., presented without qualification. If, however, the letters are "subject to" certain conditions, the investor should view them with special scrutiny. Study the audited financial statements, including footnotes. Think of it as the corporate closet. Chances are some potential skeletons have been buried there.

The investor should clearly understand that other important factors might go undisclosed. For example, a business may enjoy a strong financial position only because it fails to modernize or replace outdated facilities. In that case, the strong balance sheet will dissipate in future years as the business suffers operating losses, embarks on massive capital-expenditure programs, or both.

Look in the proxy statement disclosures for clues regarding the overreaching of management. Here the investor can examine management compensation, insider borrowing, and certain sweetheart transactions between management and the corporation it serves. Form 10-K and financial statement footnote disclosures about litigation provide investors with knowledge concerning potential losses.

OTHER CLUES TO BE FOUND

What other information might be helpful? Clues abound regarding future earnings, large cash distributions, the company's attractiveness as a takeover play, and if it could be profitably liquidated or recapitalized. The business descriptions found in disclosure materials prove helpful to investors in getting answers to these concerns.

The corporate paper trail enables a value investor to pinpoint companies to avoid. It might be a company whose financial position is so tenuous that the entire business belongs to creditors. It could be a company that is cash rich but idea poor. Or it could be a company where management's prime goal is to exploit the business and its shareholders.

Watch for Shortcomings

The investor should understand that the paper trail doesn't provide all the needed information. Unfortunately, there is no way for the average investor to look into the future or to learn a corporation's innermost secrets. For value investors, however, that particular drawback promises less serious consequences than for investors who follow other avenues.

Despite its limitations, however, the corporate paper trail is the obvious starting point in the quest for valuable information, and it provides answers to most of the questions a value investor should ask.

How to Get Documents

One way to obtain shareholder material documents is to write or call the issuer. In most instances, companies are happy to provide such information.

Another way is go directly to the Securities & Exchange Commission. The SEC has copies of documents filed on microfiche cards in its main office in Washington and (except for Schedules 13D and 14D) in its regional offices. These are made available to the public in reference rooms. The SEC also has an Internet site where most of the important shareholder documents can be downloaded from the comfort of your home or office. The site, known as EDGAR (Electronic Data Gathering, Analysis, and Retrieval System) can be reached at http://www.sec.gov/edaux/wedgar.htm.

Be Wary of What You Read

Keep in mind that annual reports are actually company sales documents. So look closely to distinguish between what is measurable and what is merely someone's opinion.

Most readers see the printed word as gospel and are content to let others analyze and interpret. That can be dangerous, whether the source is corporate documents or mass media information. The media have always dispensed a mixture of fact and opinion. Try to sift and separate what is true and measurable from what is someone's interpretation of the future. Also question the credibility of so-called experts whose names appear regularly in the financial press. The fact that *The New York Times* might imply that a person is an authority doesn't make it so. And just because someone is quoted in a major publication doesn't make that person's opinion automatically worth following.

Also keep a healthy skepticism when reading Wall Street research. Remember that analysts are known for their tendency to put an overly positive spin on some company's prospects. And keep in mind that most Wall Street research has a short-term orientation, usually focusing on a stock's prospects over the next 6 to 12 months. As we've noted in earlier chapters, that's not the time frame that matters most to a value investor.

It's helpful to read widely, of course, but always read critically. Keeping a wary eye on the information coming your way helps develop your own particular viewpoint. Pay special attention to those books and periodicals that take an untrammeled approach to investing and human nature. Even though *Value Line* and similar publications can be of great assistance, the value investor should learn to think independently.

Reports have their own biases, too, and investors must understand them. For example, *Value Line's* ranking system includes *momentum* (a growth criterion) along with basic value analysis. Value investors ignore momentum and have to adjust for the inclusion of this factor in the *Value Line* ranking system.

Digging up your own fundamental information allows you to make up your own mind based on your own value criteria. No one knows your assumptions and biases better than you. This can be vital in making buy and sell decisions.

6 CHAPTER

Checking the Fine Print

If you were buying a company outright, you would insist on a thorough understanding of its finances. Before your name went on the door, you would want to know the unvarnished truth about where the company's financial bodies are buried.

Value investors approach a company's stock as if they were buying the company itself. The primary tool for knowing the unvarnished truth about a company is financial accounting. In fact, the search for objective facts is so indispensable that accounting is the single most important analytical tool the investor can use. It is impossible to determine the necessary details about a potential investment without some knowledge of accounting.

Understandably, most investors have neither the time nor the inclination to earn a college degree in the subject. And that's fine. Although financial statement analysis can be complicated, the math skills required aren't much above the junior-high level.

What is important from the investor's point of view is what information is relevant, where to look to find that information, and what the information means. This chapter will provide answers to these fundamental questions.

THE BIG THREE

Only a few simple tests are necessary to determine whether a company is worth buying. We begin with a brief discussion of the financial accounting "big three": the balance sheet, the income statement, and the statement of cash flows. These analytical tools are indispensable in the value-investing arena, as long as you remember to read between the lines and between the international boundaries.

Balance Sheet

Also called a statement of financial condition, the balance sheet shows the nature and the amounts of a business's assets, liabilities, and stockholders' equity as of a certain date.

The most important areas of a balance sheet to examine are asset values, debt levels, and the nature of the debt, such as due dates, interest rates, and the ratio of debt to equity.

Next, explore a firm's corporate equity with an eye toward finding its true value. Is it worth more or less than stated? Perhaps the company has antiquated plants or outdated inventory. Perhaps the company has goods worth less on sale than they cost to manufacture. In other words, the investor should look behind the figures to the reality. That is the only way to calculate a company's true intrinsic value.

Ask if the numbers on the balance sheet are "real." And be skeptical; even though financial statements must be prepared according to generally accepted accounting principles (GAAP), these practices vary widely. One firm might write off assets faster than another.

Take inventory, for example. Company A might value inventory by using a method called LIFO, (last-in, first-out), while Company B might use a method called FIFO, (first-in, first-out). The method of inventory accounting used by a company can have a drastic impact on reported earnings, especially during inflationary times. These effects should be taken into account in figuring a company's intrinsic value.

The left side of the balance sheet contains the accounting figures for the total assets of the business, such as cash, accounts receivable, inventories, property, plant, and equipment. On the right side of the balance sheet are the total liabilities of the business, such as accounts payable, taxes payable, long-term debt, and the amount of the shareholders' investment in the company. As the balance sheet graphically shows, the total assets of the company equal its total liabilities plus the shareholders' investment, including retained earnings. Retained earnings are the after-tax earnings of the company that have not been paid out to shareholders in the form of dividends.

For the value investor, the balance sheet offers vital clues as to the intrinsic worth and stability of a business. If, for instance, a company's debt is three times as high as its shareholders' equity, this could be a risky company. Financial leverage is the relationship of a firm's debt to its equity. The greater the long-term debt (usually bonds), the greater the leverage. In general, industrial companies with a debt-to-equity ratio of more than 100 percent are viewed as highly leveraged. One exception to this rule is utility companies, which despite any long-term debt, often have reliable earnings and cash flow.

Goodwill is an intangible asset that can translate into considerable earning power for an operating business, yet has no dollar value when a company is liquidated. Goodwill represents such attributes as a well-respected brand or business name or strong customer relations.

In calculating depreciation or amortization, determine whether the company used historical cost or today's market value as the basis. Depreciation is the allocation of costs for fixed assets, such as plant and equipment, over a period of time that may represent the useful life of that asset. While depreciation reduces taxable income because it is deducted against earnings and the book value of an asset, it does not represent cash. Historical cost is the original or acquisition cost of an asset. Historical cost may be quite different from today's real worth of that asset. Real estate might be worth more than historical cost, while older buildings and equipment may be worth much less than the value stated on the balance sheet.

Income Statement

While the balance sheet reflects the business at a specific point in time, the income statement reflects the activities of that business over a period of time. For the investor, the income statement serves as a score card for determining the rate of return on investment.

Items on the income statement include total revenues, the cost of doing business, and the net profit for the period of time under consideration. Labor, materials, utilities, telephone, and taxes come under the heading of variable costs. These cost-of-doing-business indicators are useful in comparing a company with its competition. For example, if a company is paying taxes at a clip that is considerably lower than the corporate tax rate, you need to ask why. It could mean that the company will face a sizable tax-rate boost in the future which could negatively affect rates of return on investment over the long term.

The earnings item on the income statement lets you calculate the company's price-earnings (P/E) ratio. Be on the lookout, however, for "managed" earnings. Some companies are not above playing a bit of gamesmanship to make their bottom line look healthier than it is. For example, management could try to boost earnings during a downturn by selling off assets, such as property. Profits from the sale of assets should not be considered part of the basic earning power of a company. The investor should subtract that type of sale when basic earnings are determined.

It is also important to avoid becoming overly impressed with a company's earnings during any one year. Sophisticated investors generally get a better idea of a company's earning power by averaging profits over a fairly long period, usually five years or more. This smooths out gyrations caused by the business cycle and presents a truer picture of earning power. Also, long-term averaging neatly handles the problem of special charges and credits, since they are included in the average.

Hidden or undervalued assets can be one of the value investor's best friends. Corporate assets sometimes go unreflected on balance sheets. Even more important, the market value of these assets may be higher than the stock price itself.

Real estate frequently falls into the undervalued asset category, since land is carried at cost and buildings at depreciated cost. Suppose land prices go up? When that happens—and it often does—the actual market value can be considerably above stated book value.

Statement of Cash Flows

The statement of cash flows depicts the actual flow of cold, hard cash over a specified accounting period. Three categories that affect cash flow are operations, investments, and financing.

In analyzing the statement of cash flow, here are some questions to ponder: How much cash is available for interest payments or debt servicing? How much cash is available for reinvestment in the corporate infrastructure? How much cash will be left over for the company owners to withdraw? How much excess cash does the company generate?

Cash flow can be crucial to gauging a company's potential for success. A strong, positive cash flow usually bodes well for a company's long-term health. Cash flow statistics reveal whether operations take in more money than the firm spends over a given period of time. Businesses can lose money and still generate substantial amounts of cash. Net cash generated by the depreciation of plant and inventory on the income statement can go a long way toward keeping a company solvent in rough times.

Temporarily losing money—in an accounting sense, at least—is acceptable. Even so, beware of chronic negative cash flow. Net free working capital should be sufficient to cover at least three years of negative cash flow. Also, study company balance sheets and income statements over a period of several years to provide a more accurate picture of cash flow.

Start with net income before extraordinary items and discontinued businesses and add noncash supplements to working capital, deferred taxes, depletion, amortization, and depreciation. The Financial Accounting Standards Board requires that cash flow be divided three ways: operating, investing, and financing cash flow. This will provide a good analytic base for comparing the nature of cash flows and trends and is a welcome improvement.

Determining a company's per-share cash flow can be a useful way to determine relative value. Price-to-cash-flow ratios are calculated similarly to price-earnings ratios—by dividing the price per share of the company by the cash flow per share. Price-to-cash flow is not the only important determinant of value, of course, but it is one of the ratios value investors watch closely.

RETURN ON EQUITY

Another useful ratio that can be calculated from the financial statements is a company's return on equity, which measures the rate of return achieved on the assets invested in the business. This ratio is calculated as follows: divide net after-tax income (minus preferred dividends, if any) by common equity at the beginning of the period (minus goodwill, if any). If the company has a large deferred tax liability, you might want to add this figure to common equity, as it is an interest-free loan from the government that is used as equity.

For businesses with large amount of debt capital, return on equity will be higher than for firms without debt, all other things being equal. However, a business with considerable debt also could be riskier than one without debt, which is why simply comparing returns on equity without looking at the nature of the balance sheet could cause serious errors.

Returns on equity can be especially useful in determining overall profitability and managerial competence. In the mid-1980s, Kellogg, the world's largest cereal company, had a five-year average return on equity of 33 percent. Over the same period, Royal Nedlloyd Group, the shipping company, had an average return on equity of just 5 percent. Clearly, Kellogg was the better business.

But which was the better investment? Value investors would pick Royal Nedlloyd, because it sold for 25 percent of stockholders' equity (a 20 percent rate of return for new investors in the company at this price), while Kellogg sold at six times shareholders' equity (a 6 percent rate of return to new investors).

Note that value investors should be looking for high rates of return on equity at reasonable prices. The experienced value investor might pay more than book value (shareholders' equity) for a business generating stable and reasonably sure superior rates of return on equity. The safe course for the less knowledgeable investor, however, would be to stick to the criteria previously mentioned and buy only when the price is below book value.

STAY HOME OR GO AND LOOK?

Some value investors frequently visit companies to figuratively kick the tires. My own belief is that such visits can add to understanding, but could also subtract from objectivity.

A company's financial material usually provides all the information needed to make an informed decision. Considerable insight about management's efforts can be obtained simply by reading their ideas and plans for the business.

Here are a few items to watch for in the material: How many new products has the company developed successfully in the past few years? What percentage of last year's sales came from products recently introduced? Is the company diversified? What kind of patent protection or specific know-how protects the company from outside competition? Are they skinflints? How well do they control costs? What perks do they take? How much stock do they own? What is the trend of profit margins? What is the trend of sales and profits?

Staying home and concentrating on the objective facts is my preference, but not everyone feels the same way. If interviewing the management helps you feel more knowledgeable and comfortable about an investment, by all means pay a visit. However, be careful not to count the same positive items twice. When an investor reads and gives good marks to the published material and financial statements and then visits management and gives them good marks for the same things, the investor is counting the favorable news or numbers twice.

CONCLUSION

As tricky as financial accounting can be in the United States, it is often far more difficult abroad. That's because accounting standards and practices vary widely from country to country. In Chapter 10, you'll find a detailed breakdown of differences in accounting methods between the United States and various foreign countries.

We've now looked at financial statements, especially as they relate to domestic companies. In Chapter 7, we'll examine one of the most important questions for value investors— how to know when it's time to sell a stock.

7

CHAPTER

When to Sell, and When to Hold On

There are valid personal reasons why an investor might decide to sell common stocks. Perhaps you want to capitalize a new business, finance a new home, or need to cope with a sudden catastrophe. Selling stocks for personal rather than financial reasons falls beyond the scope of this chapter.

Our purpose here is to cover the selling motivated by a single objective: value investing. The chapter presents four reasons a value investor would find acceptable for premature selling, and also provides assistance in establishing value selling points. Other portions of this chapter address bear markets, market appreciation, and price fluctuation. Several tips and clues also have been provided regarding market uncertainty and volatility.

FOUR REASONS FOR SELLING PREMATURELY

A value investor generally sells a value stock prematurely only for these four reasons:

1. A mistake was made.
2. A better prospect has appeared (rare).
3. The security no longer qualifies as a value stock.
4. The company has participated in a merger or acquisition.

Nobody's Perfect

Even the shrewdest of investors occasionally makes a mistake. Analysis is not always perfect, so it may become apparent that a company's actual condition doesn't measure up to the original perception. Handling this type of situation calls for honesty and emotional self-control.

Above all, the ego should be kept under control. Sometimes investors fall in love with a stock. At other times, they feel foolish about being wrong and rationalize that if a "loser" can be sold at a small profit, maybe the buy wasn't so dumb after all. That's normal and natural. But it's also dangerous. Probably more money has been lost by investors who have clung to stocks until they could break even than for any other single reason. Instead of becoming disgusted or emotionally upset, review each loss with care. In that way, you'll be learning a valuable lesson and turning a negative situation into a long-term positive.

Fortunately, over the long haul, profits obtained from good value stocks should more than offset losses from such mistakes. This is particularly true if the mistakes are recognized quickly and then rectified, permitting funds to be freed up for use where substantial gains can be produced.

The Grass Is Greener Theory

A second reason value investors might sell stocks is because a better opportunity appears elsewhere. In reality this seldom occurs, but when it does, it should be acted on only when the investor is absolutely certain that a better value has actually been found.

The scenario goes like this: An investor takes a position in a well-run company that is believed to have definite value prospects. Over time, the investor discovers that such value prospects are not as attractive as some other value situation. Under those circumstances, the value investor may find it prudent to switch to a better security. But extreme care should be taken; relative value judgments are difficult. The value investor with the itchy trigger finger runs the risk of doubling the chances for error, both on the security sold and on the new security purchased.

By this time you've probably discovered a basic value principle: Once a stock has been properly selected and has withstood the test of time, it is rare that any reason exists for selling until fair value has been reached.

The Reality of Market Declines

The reader may rightly ask: "What about bear markets?" Recommendations and comments pour from the financial community to sell a stock or postpone a purchase because a bad bear market lies just over the horizon. Historically, the market runs in cycles, as will be illustrated in Chapter 12. So, if the company is really a sound investment, whatever damage a bear market might do to it over the short term will probably be more than offset during the subsequent bull market.

Further, if the investor sells a stock with the intention of rebuying it after a bear market ends, the question arises: How do you know when the market has bottomed?

In fact, experience dictates that investors rarely get back into the same shares until their price has greatly increased over the selling price. The October 1987 market crash scared many investors into selling stocks that only a few months later were substantially higher than before the decline began.

Frequently, anticipated bear markets never come. Paul Samuelson, the noted economist, once quipped that "the market has accurately called nine of the last five recessions." And William Simon, treasury secretary in the Ford administration, satirized the ability of anyone to predict the future when he said that "economists put decimal points in their forecasts to prove they have a sense of humor." Unfortunately, after you've bailed out of a good value stock for fear of a bear market that never came, you probably won't be laughing.

Stocks That No Longer Qualify

Another reason for premature selling goes to the heart of value investing itself. When a company does in fact improve its fundamentals to where the broad market has taken notice and driven up its price, it may no longer qualify as a value stock. At that point, value investors can feel justified in moving on.

A Bigger Pie Is Not Necessarily a Better Pie

Sometimes corporations acquire or merge with other companies for the right reasons. The best rationale for such a move is that the new entity can operate more efficiently, and if that is indeed the case, the shareholders of both companies benefit. In recent years, mergers within the banking sector have been generally positive developments for shareholders.

Most of the time, however, the result of corporate M&A activity is to undermine shareholder value. About half of all corporate mergers and acquisitions are later divested. Stocks of acquiring companies generally underperform their peer group for several years thereafter. A recent study by Rahul Kochlar and Parthiban David at Texas A&M University found that "takeovers are usually bad for acquiring companies, depressing their share prices and reducing their long-term profitability . . . as a rule, the higher the premium paid, the greater the losses for the acquiring firm's shareholders."[1]

But if acquisitions are bad for shareholders, why do it? Because they are frequently good for managerial self-esteem, according to another study by Matthew Hayward and Donald Hambrick at Columbia University. The researchers discovered that "acquisitions may have less to do with a cunning business calculation than with inflated managerial egos."

What should investors do if a carefully selected value stock suddenly takes on debt or uses excess cash to buy up another company? The answer is clear: The new entity you are now holding is not the same company you bought, and it almost certainly won't be the same value. Rerun the numbers on the combined company; if they don't measure up, you have all the reason you need to sell.

Look to Minimizing Risk

The three reasons noted above are the only justifications that a value investor should accept for selling stocks before they have reached a predetermined fair value. Conversely, stocks can be kept indefinitely if (1) the business grows in intrinsic value at a satisfactory rate, and (2) the market doesn't overvalue it.

That means—and this is important—if active markets stopped tomorrow, to be resumed two years hence, a value investor would not be bothered by a lack of quotes. Active trading markets are useful, but by no means essential. They can even be detrimental if their convenience motivates improper actions.

Sooner or later the fate of a value stock will be determined by the economic fate of the underlying business itself. The market may ignore a company's success for a time, but eventually that success will attract buyers. And the delayed recognition of a stock's value frequently provides the advantage of enabling the value investor to buy more shares at bargain prices.

THE CASE OF ROYAL NEDLLOYD

Here's an example of how a temporary decline in the stock price of a fundamentally sound business can actually work to the benefit of value investors.

Shares of Royal Nedlloyd Group, a Dutch shipping company, once were trading at just 25 percent of book value, two times cash flow, and six times earnings. The dividend yield was 8 percent. Those are the kinds of numbers a value investor likes to see.

Nedlloyd was initially acquired by my firm in 1985 at $35 per share. The company's price later rose to $90. Then news came that Nedlloyd would lose money in fiscal 1987 and that its dividend would be cut. That announcement was followed shortly by the October 1987 market correction. Nedlloyd's stock price dropped more than 30 percent and my clients grew doubtful. "Why didn't you sell at $90?" they asked.

The answer was simple: Even at $90 per share, Nedlloyd was still an excellent value. Our research had pegged Nedlloyd's long-term value to be $125 to $130 per share. The drop to $60 provided an opportunity to purchase more shares at 50 percent instead of 75 percent of value. Shipping rates then turned around, profitability was restored to Nedlloyd, and we eventually sold our position at $125 per share.

YARDSTICKS FOR SELL POINTS

As the Nedlloyd example illustrates, value investors establish sell points *before* shares are purchased. Unfortunately, sell points are not fixed. Frequently, the targets move in one of three directions; learning how to cope effectively with changes in sell points is extremely important.

When Should a Sell Price Be Increased?

A value investor would increase a stock's sell price any time a company reinvests earnings in its business, assuming other factors such as return on equity and the market value of assets remain unchanged. Reinvesting in a company's own business makes sense, particularly when the resulting returns are higher than if the earnings were distributed and reinvested elsewhere. When a company's fair value has been increased, the sell price also must be readjusted upward, even if the rate of return on the reinvested earnings is low or poor.

We'll use the Royal Nedlloyd Group to illustrate. For five years the company averaged a meager 5 percent return on shareholders' equity and reinvested all of its cash flow. That meant that the real value of the reinvested money declined, given just a 5 percent return. But since Royal Nedlloyd stock was priced at just 25 percent of book value, it actually generated a 20 percent rate of return for new shareholders.

Let's work the numbers. A 5 percent return on $100, of course, is $5. But a value investor buying Royal Nedlloyd shares is only paying $25 per share for those assets because the stock is selling for only one quarter of book value. At that favorable valuation, the company's 5 percent return on reinvested earnings is quite acceptable; $5 on $25 is a 20 percent return!

Here's another way of looking at it. By reinvesting the shipping company's earnings, Royal Nedlloyd receives only a 5 percent return on equity. So every $100 of reinvested earnings in that business is worth considerably less than $100. Management puts in $100, but the value of the company increases much less due to the low rate of return. But the value has increased, nonetheless.

When Does a Sell Price Remain the Same?

In the second scenario, a firm pays out its earnings and everything else remains equal. In that case, the sale price remains constant as well.

When Should a Sell Price Be Lowered?

Sell prices should be lowered if the intrinsic value of a company declines. That could happen for several reasons, including a permanent decline in corporate earning power or a decline in the rate of return on invested capital. What could cause those types of developments? Perhaps a semi-monopoly position was lost because of new competition, thereby reducing future earnings power. Or, maybe a permanent decline occurred in the value of corporate assets. In both instances, the intrinsic value of the company and the sell point of its stock would decline.

For example, take a technology company whose computers and inventories declined in value because another firm unveiled a faster model. The first company would have to unload its computers at a lower price. That, in turn, would drop the value of inventory, and the company's total value would decline along with it.

When Market Price Goes Above Fair Value

On the other hand, what happens when something catches the market's fancy and a stock price rises above the company's fair value? A good question, and a nice problem to have. It happens often, in fact, given the emotional nature of markets. But value investors remain unswayed by shifts in mass sentiment: When the fair value point is reached, value investors say thank you and good-bye, and move on in search of another undervalued company.

Value investors don't hold out for the highest price, because holding a security past the point of fair value is speculating, not investing. The margin of safety necessary to protect against future adverse developments is lost when the price is no longer right.

Value investors never reproach themselves for selling a stock too soon. You've heard the old saying: Bulls make money, bears make money, pigs get slaughtered. Value investors are neither bulls, bears, nor pigs. Value investors buy companies and hold their stocks only as long as the company's fair value is higher than its stock price.

MARKET FLUCTUATIONS AS A GUIDE

Value investors generally find market moves of little consequence. Short-term market fluctuations should become part of a value investor's thinking only on two limited occasions: when the market is so low that a company can be purchased at two-thirds of its true worth; and when a stock price approaches true value.

In other words, what the overall market does or might do is important to a value investor only because of the opportunities to buy or sell that such volatility creates.

Risk and Uncertainty

By its very nature, investing involves an element of risk; something can always go wrong. But an investor can still achieve acceptable long-term results by working to understand and minimize those risks.

Of course, not even the best investors make money all the time. Outsiders can never acquire complete knowledge of a company, regardless of how many documents are studied or how intimate the relationship with management has been. Market leadership also rotates between sectors and styles. And incorrect analysis, such as failure to account for some crucial factor, or a misjudgment of managerial skill, also plays a role. A final reason for inconsistency in results has been emphasized elsewhere in this book: The future cannot be predicted.

Sound and attractive investments sometimes fail because management has preempted the intrinsic value of their company for themselves, effecting force-out mergers or similar events when a stock's price is depressed or undervalued.

These uncertainties can't be eliminated. Rather, the goal of the value investor is to tip the risk-profit equation toward profit as much as possible.

Risk and Volatility

Many Wall Streeters fervently preach that volatility of a stock price equates to risk. As we learned earlier, that's the idea behind the statistical measurement known as beta. But value investors disagree that volatility is itself an accurate gauge of risk.

From August to October 1987, the stock market fell 36.1 percent from its high of 2,722.42. In the process, of course, the quotational values of American businesses declined. But there's a very important distinction between quotational values and actual values. The general perception is that short-term stock quotations reflect the actual value of a business. The majority of the time this is not true. Quotational values represent only what investors are willing to pay to own shares on a given day.

The wealth of the country didn't change significantly during the 1987 bear market, or even during the panic selling of shares on October 19, 1987, when the Dow fell 21 percent in one day. Actual wealth is derived from businesses themselves; it has nothing to do with daily price quotes.

Here's an example that puts the actual impact of price-quote changes into context. Let's say that Company XYZ produces widgets and has 100 shares outstanding. The $1,000 invested in the company nets an average of $100 after taxes. The stock has an intrinsic value of $10 per share.

Next, let's assume that someone wants to buy one share of XYZ, but can't find a seller. The buyer has to offer $50 before someone sells him a share. After the shares are exchanged, XYZ stock is quoted at $50. The next day, an XYZ shareholder discovers she has tax problems and needs to raise cash fast. She has to sell her XYZ share, but can get only $5 for it on that particular day. So XYZ trades at $5, or 90 percent lower than the previous quote. Yes, XYZ's stock price has declined, almost overnight, from an inflated $50 a share to a depressed $5 a share. But does that mean that the company's wealth has almost disappeared, or that shareholders' wealth has declined? No. In fact, there's no change in the actual wealth of either the company or the shareholders. The real wealth remains with a company regardless of what its stock price may be doing on a given day, or in a given year.

There's little question that market volatility has increased in recent years, mainly because of the speed of trading and the effects of a largely institutional marketplace. But price fluctuations play only a small role in value investing, and they do not equate to risk for the long-term value investor.

For value investors, the true measure of risk is not volatility in daily price quotes, but an adverse change in the intrinsic value of a business. In the long run, that's the only kind of volatility than can hurt you. The idea, then, is to keep an eye on the company and not the stock price.

And what if a company's stock price declines even though its intrinsic value is stable or increases? In that case, value investors buy more shares. Over the long term, investing in equities at reasonable prices on a diversified basis provides a higher rate of return than that available from any competing asset class. But to make those returns, you have to avoid the temptation to panic and sell because of temporarily declining stock prices.

CONCLUSION

In this chapter, we presented several guidelines and procedures for the eventual sale of value stocks. We also looked at some acceptable reasons for selling a value stock prematurely. Combined with information presented in earlier chapters, we've now covered the rationale for value investing, how to pick value stocks, and when to sell them. Next, let's turn our attention to where to find value opportunities. We'll start by exploring foreign markets, an especially fertile breeding ground for value stocks.

NOTES

1. Rahul Kochlar and Parthiban David, in *The Economist* (August 12, 1995).

PART THREE

LEARNING TO THINK GLOBALLY

8

CHAPTER

Why Go Overseas?

It's not easy for Americans to look at the world as a playground of investment opportunity. From the day we're born until the day we die, we receive the same messages over and over again: America is the best place on earth; preserve America; buy American. The messages work, at least in terms of keeping U.S. investors from looking abroad.

But the media message—packaged to a large degree by corporate America and reinforced by a steady diet of images showing world disorder—is a story filled with misconception and misinformation.

For example, a West Coast company specializing in food photography stepped onto the "Buy American" platform by declaring it would no longer purchase film from a Japanese-based company. On the surface, this move positioned the photography firm nicely with the media and the community. On closer examination, however, it was discovered that the

Japanese-based company had a substantial operation in the United States employing thousands of Americans, while the American company did an outstanding business in Japan, providing steady income to a large number of Japanese distributors.

The truth is, it's comfortable to think American and support America. Certainly, the United States is the most successful and powerful nation in the world. What we often fail to realize, however, is how truly integrated the economic world has become, with the daily interweaving of industry and technology, manufacturing and science. We've learned to accept without question the international brand names on our transportation, telecommunications, banking, and electronics systems. What we have not learned to do with any consistency is to think beyond our borders—to think globally—when it comes to investment opportunities.

A WORLD WITHOUT BOUNDARIES

It's easy to see why Americans take an overly provincial approach to investing. Human nature drives us to keep within known boundaries. At the same time, the world seems to grow more fragmented hour by hour. Understandably, we're sometimes reluctant to place our trust and dreams in the markets of countries that might seem better suited to wild-eyed speculators than prudent investors.

The real story is quite different. Foreign stocks, when evaluated by experienced, professional investment strategists, can be a safe, reliable, and profitable place to invest long-term money.

There are three overriding reasons for diversifying your holdings to include a significant amount of foreign stocks. First, overseas is where most of the businesses are located. Second, overseas is where much of the return has been. And third, overseas is where you can get the most significant diversification. Following are brief summaries of each of these key reasons for owning foreign stocks.

Opportunity

Two-thirds of the world's equity value is now located outside the United States, yet less than 10 percent of American investors buy individual foreign stocks. Domestic investors usually shy away from foreign bourses because of uncertainties about how to evaluate markets and companies. After all, America is the land of blue chips and fast risers, old favorites and high-yield comers. But restricting potential investments to just one-third of the world's opportunities is far too limiting. More importantly, it's self-defeating. By closing off your investment world at the U.S. border, you give up the opportunity to buy into seven of the ten largest insurance companies in the world; eight out of ten of the largest chemical companies; eight out of the ten largest electronics companies; eight of the ten largest automobile manufacturers; nine of the ten largest machinery companies; nine of the ten largest utilities; and the world's ten largest banks.

Return

Since the early 1980s, a unique confluence of favorable demographic trends and persistent disinflation has powered American equities to a series of record highs. Yet despite the impressive recent returns, foreign stock markets have done even better over the long haul. When measured in U.S. dollars, the average American stock has underperformed 13 of the 21 developed equity markets comprising the Morgan Stanley Capital International Europe Australasia Far East Index (EAFE) since 1970. As of year-end 1996, MSCI's U.S. Index stood at 701, compared to 1173 for the EAFE (base: January 1, 1970 = 100).[1]

Diversification

Putting all your money in one country makes about as much portfolio sense as putting all your money in one industry or one company. Rational investors diversify as much as possible, and cross-border investing is an important part of that strategy.

Unfortunately, to many American investors, the phrase "foreign stock" is virtually synonymous with risk. Images of sword-flashing dictators, currency devaluations, and third-world poverty come easily to mind. And yes, historical evidence does confirm that foreign equity markets *in general* are more volatile than those in the United States. But risk can be overcome through diversification on a worldwide basis, and through long-term investments in companies whose stock is undervalued in relation to the real value of the business. (Remember the basic principle from earlier chapters: No single factor lowers risk more than buying a company at a favorable price.) By diversifying their holdings to include carefully selected value stocks in several foreign markets, investors lower the risks associated with both the domestic and foreign portions of their portfolios.

METHODS OF RISK ASSESSMENT

Besides gaining access to many of the world's best business values—and the returns that flow to the owners of those values—buying foreign stocks lowers overall risk by spreading around exposure to various economies and markets.

In this section we discuss the relationship of simultaneous investment returns in global markets. We also consider methods of risk assessment used by professional investors, including short-term volatility and comparing a business's value with its stock price. As value investors, we favor the latter method.

International Volatility and the Value Investor

Volatility is the tendency of a security's market value to fluctuate sharply up or down in the short term. For traders who want to sell off their portfolios at a moment's notice, volatility and risk are roughly equivalent. But for value investors, who don't have the urge to liquidate their portfolios in a nanosecond, volatility has its limitations as a measure of risk. In the long term, we consider volatility less significant than the value of the business and the price you pay for that business.

Despite these reservations, a discussion of volatility merits inclusion in this chapter for the following reasons:

- Many investors are volatility-averse and cannot tolerate dramatic price fluctuations in their portfolio.
- In the academic community, volatility is the only quantifiable measure of risk and is extensively cited in studies of risk analysis.
- Empirical studies showing the lack of correlation between U.S. and nondomestic stock markets use portfolio beta as a yardstick. Portfolio beta measures a portfolio's relative volatility against overall market movement. The lack of correlation suggests that real diversification will occur if a portfolio includes a mix of securities from both U.S. and non-U.S. markets. We agree that international diversification is a sound investment strategy, and the lack of international market correlations bolsters that strategy.

Modern portfolio theory is a quantitative approach to investing that tends to equate volatility with risk. Proponents of this method emphasize the statistical relationships among the various securities comprising an overall stock portfolio. Unlike value investors, quantitative analysts tend to focus on technical analysis and statistical relationships among stocks rather than bottom-up analysis of individual businesses.

Adherents of modern portfolio theory quantify the relationship between risk and return, use asset allocation to create a mix of bonds and equities in the portfolio, and stress diversification as a means of reducing risk.

Beta as a Measure of Volatility

Beta is a measure of how price movements of an individual stock correspond with movements in the overall market. A beta of 1.00 suggests that the movement of the individual security is in tandem with the movement of the U.S. market. (The S&P 500 Index has a beta coefficient of 1.00.) Any security with a higher beta is said to be more volatile than the market and will fluctuate more in price than the overall market. Any security with a lower beta is said to be less volatile than the market. For example, a beta of 1.20 suggests that a 1.00 percent move in the S&P 500 will correspond to a 1.2 percent move in that individual security.

According to the academic theory of capital markets, the higher the beta, the greater the risk and the greater the potential reward. Conversely, the lower the beta, the lower the risk and the lower the potential reward.

Modern portfolio theorists contend that the compensation for increased risk is the potential for greater investment profits. Since lowering the beta lowers the risk, these academics favor the inclusion of low-beta bonds in a portfolio to dampen the volatility of higher-beta equities.

Standard Deviation and Lumpy Returns

Standard deviation is a measure of the dispersion of returns around the average return. The greater the standard deviation, the greater the volatility of a particular investment, portfolio, or market.

Investments with high standard deviations tend to produce uneven returns. Treasury bills, on the other hand, have a fairly narrow standard deviation and therefore exhibit relatively low volatility. The rational long-term investor, of course, would not object to lumpy, short-term results, as long as the returns were considerably greater than smooth returns available from Treasury bills.

There is a caveat, however. If you are a volatility-averse investor, a run of dismal prices could be hazardous to your long-term financial health. If your fear of fluctuating market values or need for short-term cash could push you into selling out at low prices, it's best to dampen the volatility of your portfolio as much as possible. Recognize your own tolerance for volatility, and structure your portfolio accordingly. That's preferable to making multiple selling errors based on fear.

Depending on your view of volatility, the aftermath of the 1987 stock market crash in the United States was either a warning or an opportunity. Some people, haunted by the specter of fluctuating prices, vowed that they would never again invest in common stocks. Meanwhile, volatility-tolerant value investors went on a shopping spree for bargain-priced companies. As it turned out, those bargain-hunting value investors were right. As of the ninth anniversary of the crash in 1996, the average U.S. stock had appreciated 269 percent from its October 19, 1987, low.

Correlation

The best of all possible worlds is a low-beta asset that boosts portfolio return. Studies suggest that if you include foreign stocks in a U.S.-only portfolio, at worst you maintain the equivalent rate of return, but with less standard deviation.

Adding foreign stocks lowers your portfolio's overall risk while maintaining its reward potential because American and overseas markets are not perfectly correlated. In other words, when one market zigs, another market often zags.

We know that at any given time the world's stock markets may well be out of sync with one another. For example, while the S&P 500 Index returned a mere 5 percent in 1989, the Japanese stock market enjoyed a 43 percent gain. When the S&P fell by 5 percentage points in 1982, Sweden's market rose by 43 percent. The notoriously volatile Hong Kong stock market topped all performers for three years in the 1979 to 1988 time frame. But in 1982 it tumbled 42 percent, while the S&P expanded by 21 percent.

Empirical evidence supports the anecdotal observation that global markets do not necessarily move in tandem with the U.S. market. These studies depict the extent of co-movement between markets, i.e., how closely the movement of one market parallels the movement of another.

The co-movement, or correlation coefficient, is a statistical measure of the extent to which one market's movement can be explained by the movement of another market. Historically, for example, price movements in the Swiss market can be statistically explained by price movements in the German market. Therefore, these two markets are highly correlated, and not much diversification benefit is derived from investing in both markets.

On the other hand, there is very little statistical evidence to suggest that movements in the Swiss market explain movements in the Mexican market. They move independently, are therefore not highly correlated, and can offer the benefits of diversification to the investor who buys both Swiss and Mexican issues.

The correlation coefficient is measured on a scale ranging from positive to negative and generally ranging from +1.0 to −1.0. A +1.00 correlation between two markets means that they are moving in lock step; if market A moves up 1 percent, so does market B. A − 1.00 correlation between two markets means that they are moving in totally opposite directions, but by equal amounts; if market A moves up 1 percent, market B moves down 1 percent. A zero correlation signifies no relationship whatsoever.

The purpose of tracking a market's correlation coefficient is to maximize the risk-reduction benefits of diversification. If half of an investor's assets are in American stocks and the remaining portion is concentrated in markets with a high correlation to the U.S., whatever diversification is achieved will probably not translate into any meaningful risk reduction. Minimizing risk requires diversifying into markets with low correlation coefficients.

The coefficient of correlation for EAFE versus the U.S. is 0.49, which indicates that the movements of American stocks and a diversified basket of foreign equities are not closely correlated. This suggests that good diversification benefits can be achieved by investing part of your portfolio overseas.

Reasons for Low Correlations

Low correlations between various equity markets result from any of a number of factors. The most common reason is nonsynchronous economic cycles. For example, one country's economy could be falling into recession while another nation's economy may just be gathering steam. Politics, fiscal policy, and popular sentiment may also come into play to create different economic landscapes from one market to another. Historically, investors who diversify overseas have benefited from higher returns and lower volatility.

Today, however, some investors believe that global correlations are increasing. The integration of the world's economies and the increased cross-border flow of information and capital have reinforced this belief. The theory sounds plausible, but is it true?

We looked at each rolling five-year period since 1971, using two benchmark indices, the MSCI EAFE and the Standard & Poor's 500, as proxies for the foreign and U.S. markets, respectively. The results (see Exhibit 8-1) indicate that there is no discernible trend toward increasing correlation between overseas and U.S. markets.

Although the globalization of markets is driving new technologies and approaches to investing, some of the basic principles remain unchanged. The more diversified a portfolio is, the less likely it is to fall prey to extreme fluctuations.

E X H I B I T   8 - 1

EAFE vs. S&P 500 5-Year Rolling Correlation

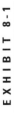

ea-correl	
Mar 77	0.74
Mar 78	0.72
Mar 79	0.74
Mar 80	0.40
Mar 81	0.52
Mar 82	0.72
Mar 83	0.83
Mar 84	0.71
Mar 85	0.67
Mar 86	0.62
Mar 87	0.41
Mar 88	0.58
Mar 89	0.55
Mar 90	0.53
Mar 91	0.62
Mar 92	0.66
Mar 93	0.68
Mar 94	0.67
Mar 95	0.68
Mar 96	0.24
Mar 97	(0.12)

Correlation between the U.S. and Int'l Markets has actually been declining and is at its lowest level in the past 20 years.

The bottom line is that overseas diversification still makes sense for investors looking to reduce volatility.

DIVERSIFY TO LOWER RISK AND ENHANCE REWARD

Exhibit 8-2 shows how global diversification can reduce risk and increase reward. To obtain this particular curve, we plotted the performance and volatility of various portfolios comprised of a mix of S&P 500 and EAFE equities. We used the 25-year period ended December 31, 1996.

In the graph in Exhibit 8-2, the bottom of the curve represents a portfolio that is 100 percent invested in domestic stocks. As you move up the curve, the proportion of U.S. stocks in the portfolio decreases. The top of the curve represents a portfolio that is 100 percent invested in the EAFE, or nondomestic stocks. The annualized return (Y axis) represents the geometric average of the annual return for a particular asset mix.

There are several points of interest on this curve:

- The portfolio consisting of exclusively U.S. stocks has the lowest average annual return.
  Unfortunately, this allocation model is far too common among U.S. investors.
- The portfolio that produces the lowest annual variance (standard deviation) consists of 70 percent domestic and 30 percent foreign stocks.
  Volatility-averse investors would favor this allocation.
- The portfolio that includes a mix of 45 percent U.S. stocks and 55 percent foreign stocks equaled the variance or volatility of the 100 percent U.S. portfolio but with an average of 1.5 percent extra return per year. This is the "free lunch" that efficient-market believers say is unattainable: greater reward for no greater level of variance or "risk."

E X H I B I T 8 - 2

25-Year Risk/Return Tradeoff (Ending 12/31/96)

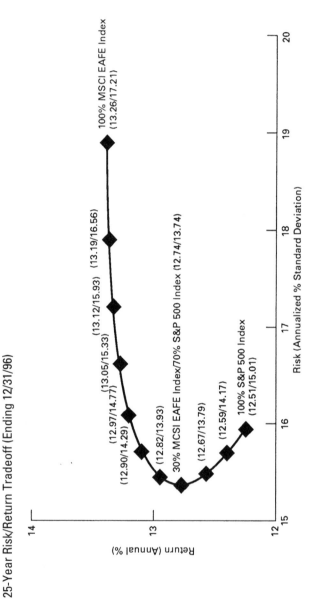

Source: Frank Russell Company.

- The portfolio that produces the highest annual return consists of 100 percent foreign equities. The investor seeking to maximize return without concern for volatility would favor this allocation.

If a 45–55 split between U.S. and foreign equities produces the best risk-adjusted return, evidence suggests that American investors have some serious catching up to do on the international side of their portfolios. Currently, U.S. pension funds have slightly less than 10 percent of assets in nondomestic issues. Although pension fund managers are finally moving in the right direction, they are moving too slowly to take advantage of what the international investment market has to offer. Remember, nearly two-thirds of the world's market capitalization is now located outside the United States.

We recommend that institutional investors dedicate 25 percent to 30 percent of the stock portion of their portfolios to international equities. And as the world's economies become even more interdependent over the next decade, increasing the foreign portion to as high as 40 percent would be in order.

FACTORS IN SUPERIOR FOREIGN EQUITY RETURNS

It's no coincidence that foreign equities have generally beaten the return of U.S. stocks over the last quarter century. Following are brief overviews of secular trends that have underwritten the superior return from non-U.S. markets in the past and are likely to continue to do so in coming years.

Growth

Higher economic growth rates in foreign countries support the higher performance numbers in overseas equity markets. Between 1974 and 1990, the U.S. economy grew by

an average of 2.6 percent per year while world GDP was
growing by 3.0 percent. During the same period, low- and
middle-income Asian nations were increasing real GDP by
6.8 percent annually.

The faster growth overseas is expected to continue.
According to the World Bank, real GDP in high-income
nations such as the United States is projected to increase
by just 2.9 percent annually over the next decade, compared
with 3.5 percent for the overall global economy, 3.8 percent
in Latin America, and nearly 8 percent in parts of Asia.[2]

Privatization

The accelerating global trend toward free enterprise has
begun to eliminate many of the inefficiencies caused by
overzealous government intervention and has paved the
way for remarkable growth rates in both developing and
developed countries.

The process of converting previously state-owned
businesses to the private sector is known as "privatization."
The rationale for privatization is to inject increased competition into an economy, since government, by nature, is a
monopoly. Competition almost always provides services
and products that are not only cheaper, but of higher quality. From the investor's viewpoint, privatization also provides more investment opportunities, since stocks of more
companies are available. While the more obvious examples
of privatization are taking place in formerly Communist
nations such as Russia and Poland, large-scale privatiza-
tions are also going forward in Latin America, Western
Europe, and Asia.

Pro-Business Policies

Besides privatization, many foreign governments have
taken other measures to aid the development of their
economies. Among the more significant is the liberalization

of direct foreign investment, a change that has enabled companies to obtain the necessary capital to expand and modernize their production facilities. Between 1990 and 1994, private long-term capital flows (a category that includes foreign direct investment) grew by roughly 40 percent in Latin America and the Caribbean and by more than 20 percent throughout Asia.[3]

Technology

Increases in the speed of technology transfers also have helped many countries modernize their industries and increase productivity. Whereas most of the industries in the United States and Japan have forged new technologies, this is not true for most foreign countries. With new technologies becoming increasingly easier to obtain, foreign markets have the potential to continue outperforming the United States market. By tapping into this potential, the international investor can greatly increase returns.

Trade

Global commerce is growing in real terms at the rate of 6 to 8 percent per year. As the World Bank noted in a recent overview of global economic trends, "During 1985–94 the ratio of world trade to GDP rose three times faster than in the previous ten years and nearly twice as fast as in the 1960s, the celebrated 'golden age' of rapid world growth and trade expansion."[4] Increasingly, governments are realizing that lowering trade barriers ultimately improves their economies, even if previously protected industries are at least temporarily harmed. And as trade barriers are removed, products are free to cross borders, allowing for the most efficient utilization of resources. That's always good for the global economy and, by extension, for global investors.

EMERGING MARKETS

The difference between "developed" and "emerging" markets is a function of the size of the underlying economy. According to the World Bank, markets considered to be emerging are those in nations with per capita gross domestic products of $9,000 or less. (Some countries with larger economies may still be considered as emerging if capital markets are small.) The average per capita GDP of the roughly 170 nations classified as "emerging" is a little over $1,000. By comparison, per capita GDP in the U.S. is over $25,000.

Currently, there are 14 "major" emerging-market countries. Together, markets in these nations account for over 75 percent of the Morgan Stanley Capital International Emerging Markets Free Index (EMF). Nearly 45 percent of the index is represented by Malaysia, South Africa, and Brazil. Countries considered "major" by MSCI include Argentina, Brazil, Chile, India, Indonesia, Israel, Korea, Malaysia, Mexico, the Philippines, Portugal, South Africa, South Korea, and Thailand.

Following are several reasons to include stocks in developing or emerging economies:

• **Performance.** From 1988 through 1995, the average emerging-market stock outperformed its U.S. counterpart by about 250 percent.

• **Rapid growth.** Many of the fastest growing countries in the world are home to emerging markets. According to the World Bank, the economies of emerging-market nations grew more than twice as fast as those of the U.S. and other foreign developed countries between 1985 and 1994.

• **Population.** The nearly 5 billion people living in developing nations account for more than 85 percent of the world's population.

• **Undercapitalized markets.** Output from developing economies represents roughly 22 percent of global GDP, yet emerging markets are capitalized at just 9 percent of the aggregate value of the world's equity markets. Those figures suggest considerable room for share-price appreciation, even without above-average economic growth.

• **Improving liquidity.** In the past, emerging markets were generally illiquid and restrictive of foreign portfolio investment. As developing economies become more dependent on capital to fund improvements in infrastructure, emerging markets will increasingly be opened to foreign investment.

• **Potential.** The full economic potential of many emerging markets is only now beginning to be realized. In Latin American, a shift in policy away from import substitution and toward free trade is designed to strengthen international competitiveness. Import substitution is an inward-looking policy that seeks to develop a protected domestic market through the use of high tariffs and government incentives to supply products that were imported previously. Such policies result in inefficient industries that are reliant on costly government intervention.

• **Market Inefficiencies.** Since emerging markets are generally the least-researched segment of the equity universe, they can be a great source for undiscovered values. As a result, the international investor is able to get in on the ground floor on many solid businesses and profit from emerging nations' typically above-average growth rates.

• **Flexibility.** Another benefit of investing in emerging countries is their ability to adjust to periods of expansion and contraction. This is a direct result of minimal wage and employment restrictions. If the economy of an emerging country is experiencing a slowdown, companies are better able to adapt by adjusting production capacity than are companies in large industrialized countries, which often have strict minimum wage legislation and employment protection laws.

• **Diversification.** Investments in emerging markets usually diversify a portfolio to a greater extent than even traditional EAFE-style international allocation. That's because the equity markets in emerging countries have substantially lower correlations with the United States than do those of developed countries. Including emerging markets in an international portfolio decreases volatility and offers great growth prospects.

To be sure, investments in emerging markets carry risks. In general, the risks are only a somewhat heightened version of those found in developed foreign countries. Each of the important risk factors will be explained in greater detail in Chapter 10.

Despite the risks, emerging-market securities offer important advantages that cannot be attained in developed markets. In modest and carefully selected dosages, investments in emerging markets can actually help to lower a portfolio's overall volatility while enhancing its return.

Market Inefficiencies

As noted earlier, one of the strongest arguments for investing in foreign countries is the relatively inefficient nature of their markets.

Market efficiency is the extent to which information about a specific company is publicly known and reflected in its stock price. Even the highly regulated U.S. equities market isn't very efficient, despite a mandated system of quarterly reports, computer-generated information, and hordes of analysts. Those uniquely human factors—fear and greed—often distort an issue's pricing, particularly over the short term.

Market inefficiencies in the global marketplace, on the other hand, result from a combination of reduced empirical research and fewer analysts searching for underpriced securities. But that's good: Fewer people means less competition for values. The recent decline in transaction costs in many foreign markets have made these inefficiencies even more attractive. The international investor should seek out market inefficiencies and uncover the stocks that are selling below their fair market value.

Less Competition

In most businesses, including the business of investing, lack of competition often leads to higher profits. It's easier to find bargains when there are fewer bargain hunters out and around. We find that the majority of investors in non-U.S. equities favor growth-investing strategies. That leaves value investors in a dominant minority position, with wide latitude to pursue opportunities overseas.

It's a different story in the U.S., where there's considerably more elbowing than there used to be for undervalued domestic stock. Value investing has attracted plenty of converts over the years—particularly from 1975 to 1985, when top value investors easily outperformed their growth-oriented colleagues. Outside the United States, however, the concept of value investing is virtually unknown.

INTERNATIONAL BARGAIN HUNTING

Diversification makes sense, regardless of your investment style. And just as you shouldn't limit yourself to a single industry, you shouldn't limit yourself to a single country. If you were looking for bargains in the communications sector a few years ago Compañía de Telefónos de Chile (CTC) was considerably cheaper than any comparable U.S. stock; at one time, Chile's phone company was trading at five times earnings. Nestle and Heineken were attractively priced compared with U.S. food stocks, and Sandoz enjoyed a similar position in the pharmaceutical field. In the automotive sector, Volkswagen formerly traded at 1.25 times cash flow, versus four times cash flow for Chrysler and General Motors.

Value investors seek out these price anomalies, which are often irrational. Valuations in Japan trading in the early 1990s—P/E ratios of 40 to 50 times earnings and earnings yields of barely 1 percent—made no sense. For that matter, Japan trading at three times earnings in 1963 made no sense either. At present, the combination of less empirical research and fewer analysts seeking underpriced securities in non-U.S. markets is a boon for the value investor.

But don't expect pricing irregularities to last forever. International accounting standards and worldwide electronic trading will eventually eliminate many of these market inefficiencies. However, rationality will never fully determine market values. The gamut of human emotions—from greed and enthusiasm to fear and pessimism—can alter perceived or short-term values and send prices spinning up or down.

Choose the Company, Not the Country

As proponents of a bottom-up investment style, we never had much use for the strategy that allocates worldwide stock purchases according to country. Bottom-up investors choose the stock first; where the company happens to be domiciled plays a role in the decision-making process only to the extent that prudent managers should be cautious about becoming overweighted in the securities of any single country.

We're more interested in hunting down individual stocks with promising fundamentals and cheap prices than we are in assessing general economic trends. Our assumption is that individual companies can be welcome additions to our portfolio—even in an industry or a country that is not performing well overall at the moment.

Top-down investors take a different approach. Top-down strategies—currently the most prevalent among international money managers—are based on country allocations. "Top-downers" begin by choosing the countries or local economies that meet their criteria; then they pick the stocks.

Active Management Adds Value

When you think about it, allocation-by-country is just another name for indexing, although you're doing it on a worldwide basis. And indexing, we believe, is an approach unworthy of a talented investment manager. Instead of making reasoned choices, you're buying and selling a basket of stocks to match the performance of some broad-based index that mirrors the market as a whole.

Indexing is the technique used by institutional investors when they buy all the equities in a given stock index, such as the S&P 500 Index. For example, when Reebok was added to the S&P 500, its value rose in one day by more than $70 million because so many fund managers were obligated to buy it.

Many international fund managers base their investments on the market capitalization weighting of the world's stock market indexes, such as Morgan Stanley's Capital International EAFE index, which measures the performance of European, Australasian, and Far Eastern markets. This style of investing ignores the value of the individual businesses within the chosen countries.

During the 1980s, the EAFE index outperformed the U.S. indexes. Fund managers with top-down styles willingly "bought" the EAFE index, even when it meant buying Japanese stocks at 60 times earnings. (Today, Japan represents roughly one-third of the capitalization-weighted EAFE.) In 1992, with the Tokyo market at a mere 50 percent of its former value, that indexing philosophy revealed itself for what it was: a failed attempt at macroeconomic forecasting. That it failed was hardly surprising; neither countries nor companies are perpetual growth machines.

One consequence of the inefficient nature of foreign markets is that an even greater premium is put on active management. In an article published in *Pension Management*, authors Christopher Carabell and Elizabeth DeLalla write

that "of the major asset classes, international equity affords
the broadest potential for active managers. None of the criteria used in assessing the relative merits of active vs. passive—viable indices, available information, management
fees and transaction costs—strongly favor indexation when
investing abroad. Active international management has the
additional advantage of multidimensional investment opportunities, including country and stock selection . . . Taken
together, these factors clearly demonstrate why international
equity should contain the most active approaches in the
management structure."[5]

Indexing implies a macroeconomic forecast, and value
investors do not forecast. As Warren Buffett once observed,
"We've long felt that the only value of stock forecasters is to
make fortune-tellers look good."[6] Value investors try to buy
what they can measure today at a discount from its current
worth. The only thing riskier than predicting the near-term
economic outlook for a company is predicting the near-term
economic outlook for an entire regional marketplace. We appreciate the earnings potential of the world's emerging markets. But we wouldn't even give these markets a second look if
their shares were trading at above-average P/E multiples.

Look for Underperforming Markets

Value bargains are rarely found in strong markets. A good
rule for value investors is to research stock markets that have
reacted adversely for a year or so. The Netherlands was a
likely place to look in 1987, when its stock market was at the
bottom of the world's performance list. One of our picks at
that time was Akzo N.V., which produces coatings, fibers,
and pharmaceuticals. It was trading at five times earnings,
three times cash flow, and 60 percent of book value, with a
dividend yield of 7 percent.

Contrast this with Dow Chemical, which was trading at
twice book value and seven times cash flow, with a P/E ratio

of 12 and a dividend yield of 3 percent. By not restricting our search to U.S. markets, we were able to find a company that was somewhat equivalent in size and product line to a Dow Chemical Company, but trading at roughly half the price of the American giant. From 1988 to 1992, Dow returned 4.6 percent per year, including dividends. Akzo's annualized return for that same period was 21.2 percent.

In evaluating Akzo, analysts treated the company as if it were exclusively a producer of low-profit, bulk commodity products. In reality, Akzo manufactures several successful pharmaceutical products, including the best-selling oral contraceptive in Europe. This low-dose contraceptive, notable for its absence of side-effects, will eventually be introduced into the U.S. marketplace.

The Forgotten Ones

In the quest for international value, it also pays to research industries that are overlooked, are in a cyclical decline, or are reasonably priced throughout the world. Once you have found an inexpensive sector, search out the world's least expensive buys within that sector. Elf Aquitaine, for instance, selling at 7.5 times earnings in 1991, was easily the cheapest major integrated oil company in the world.

Telmex was a value standout in the telecommunications field. If you bought Mexico's phone company when it was selling at $1 per share and held the stock for nine years, you realized 57 times your original investment. Its $1 cost represented three times earnings, 25 percent of book value, and one time cash flow.

When Talk Was Cheap in Chile

Yet another value opportunity was Compañía de Telefónos de Chile (CTC), which traded on the New York Stock Exchange at five times earnings and 80 percent of book value, with a dividend yield of over 12 percent. That was in July 1990, when U.S. phone companies were trading at approximately 13 times earnings and twice book value, with dividend yields of between 5 and 6 percent. While the U.S. companies were growing at 12 percent a year on average, CTC was experiencing annual growth rates of 25 percent. And unlike U.S. phone companies, CTC served a developing country with an underdeveloped telephone infrastructure.

Making the stock an even better deal was the attitude of Chile's government, which was strongly committed to economic growth and a hands-off policy toward private enterprise.

We bought CTC at $15 a share. Seven months later, the stock had been discovered by the rest of the world—and had tripled in value.

Global Beer Versus Home Brew

Anheuser-Busch's Budweiser beer may be popular in the United States, but has little international appeal. In 1991, whether you were a beer drinker or a value investor, Heineken was a headier brew than Bud. At that time, however, Anheuser-Busch—the world's largest beer maker—was trading at 21 times trailing earnings and 13 times cash flow. Heineken, a Dutch company and the world's number-two brewer, was trading at 12 times trailing earnings and seven times cash flow. In 1991, Anheuser-Busch sold some 2.5 billion gallons of suds, including the Budweiser label, while Heineken came in a distant second with 1.32 billion.

In 1990, valuations in the Dutch stock market were generally cheaper than those in U.S., and Heineken's price per share reflected that situation. When we began buying Heineken in 1991, we appreciated its comparatively low P/E ratio in the international beverage sector. We also appreciated the stock's growth potential.

The Dutch brewer, unlike Anheuser-Busch, is a global player with sales in 150 countries and 90 global production facilities. Anheuser-Busch, with most of its sales in the U.S., serves a declining market.

Just about the only growth niche in the shrinking U.S. beer market is for premium brews. Heineken, a quality product with international cachet, fills that bill nicely, while the majority of Anheuser-Busch products still seem targeted toward a blue-collar market. Subsequently, Heineken's value has been recognized, and the stock now sells at a higher valuation than Busch.

And what did we do while the global marketplace was only gradually coming to recognize Heineken's superior value? We waited patiently, of course, and held the stock for as long as the process of recognition took. No timetables, no rush. In the words of the master himself, Warren Buffett: "We continue to make more money when snoring than when active."[7]

CONCLUSION

This chapter has demonstrated the unique opportunities that global investing offers the value investor. The propitious way that foreign markets and value stocks complement each other also was discussed in a study by Rex A. Sinquefeld, published in the *Financial Analysts Journal.* Writes Sinquefeld: "International value stocks and international small stocks diversify U.S. portfolios more than EAFE. In fact, a sensible reason to diversify internationally is to 'load up' on value stocks and small stocks without concentrating in one geographic region."[8]

In Chapter 9, we'll show you the various methods for buying and selling international value stocks.

NOTES

1. *Barron's* (January 6, 1997), p. MW57.
2. "Global Economic Prospects and the Developing Countries." (The World Bank, 1996), p. 76.

3. Ibid., p. 85.

4. Ibid., p. 1.

5. Christopher C. Carabell and Elizabeth L. DeLalla, "Index vs. Active Investment," *Pension Management* (April 1995), pp. 11, 38.

6. James P. Miller and Robert L. Rose, "Buffett Turns Wary on Rise of Stock Prices," *The Wall Street Journal* (March 17, 1997), p. C1.

7. Ibid., p. 17.

8. Rex A. Sinquefeld, in *Financial Analysts Journal* (January / February 1996).

9

CHAPTER

How to Invest in Foreign Stocks

When value investors go shopping overseas, they have three methods of buying equities: American Depositary Receipts, direct purchase of ordinary foreign shares, and prepackaged investments such as closed- and open-end mutual funds. In this chapter, we will discuss each of these means to gain access to foreign markets. We also will offer tips on choosing an international private investment manager.

AMERICAN DEPOSITARY RECEIPTS

American Depositary Receipts (ADRs) first appeared on the investment scene in 1927, when J.P. Morgan Bank issued receipts for the British retailer Selfridge Stores. Prior to the 1980s, ADRs were primarily used by foreign companies to create stock-purchase plans for their U.S.-based employees.

The receipts also helped to cut through red tape in the buying and settling of foreign stocks for pension plans. It wasn't until recently, however, that overseas companies began to use ADRs as a means of raising capital.

Today, ADRs are popular among foreign companies issuing stock and investors seeking more direct access to non-U.S. markets. Over 1,300 ADRs from roughly 40 countries trade in the United States, and the capitalization of the ADR market has tripled since the mid-1980s.

What Is an ADR?

An ADR is a certificate that is issued by a U.S. depository (usually a bank) and that represents underlying foreign shares of stock. The holder can convert the certificate (ADR) into the foreign stock and is entitled to the dividends and capital gains of the underlying shares.

Like any domestic U.S. stock, an ADR is purchased with U.S. dollars, pays dividends in U.S. dollars, and is listed on U.S. exchanges or traded over-the-counter. The Securities and Exchange Commission views an ADR as a negotiable U.S. asset. But while ADRs are traded like domestic securities, they are actually foreign shares and are affected by international currency fluctuations. For example, the price of a Nintendo ADR trading on the New York Stock Exchange will precisely track the price of Nintendo stock on the Tokyo exchange, *after adjusting for changes in the dollar-yen relationship.* The impact of currency fluctuations on ADR prices is a financial fact of life that is often overlooked, even by experienced market watchers. We will explain currency fluctuations and their effects on foreign investments in Chapter 10.

Types of ADRs

There are three types of ADRs: unsponsored, sponsored, and exchange-listed (a special category of sponsored ADRs).

Unsponsored ADRs

Some ADRs are created without the consent of the underlying company by banks that see a profitable market for the company's shares. These unsponsored issues may be handled by more than one bank, and the holder is responsible for paying the bank's fees.

Despite their relatively large share of the overall ADR market, unsponsored ADRs are probably a vanishing breed. They are becoming less popular with investors because company information and performance reports can be relatively difficult to obtain. When it comes to generating investor interest in a foreign company, the lack of SEC regulation for unsponsored ADRs is a powerful negative.

Sponsored ADRs

Sponsored ADRs are handled through a single bank and are typically accompanied by a stock exchange listing and contractual agreement between the company and the depository bank. The foreign company picks up most of the bank's fees.

Since the sponsored ADR complies with many of the SEC's reporting requirements, the individual investor can easily acquire the information needed to make a prudent buying decision. But from the issuing company's point of view, sponsored ADRs are expensive.

All ADRs trading on the New York and American exchanges must be sponsored. Although the NASDAQ stock market prefers sponsored ADRs, they are not considered mandatory.

Sponsored ADRs are increasingly popular with investors because they provide a greater flow of information than unsponsored ADRs.

Exchange-Listed ADRs

The exchange-listed ADR provides more and better information to the holder than either nonsponsored or nonexchange-sponsored receipts. To qualify for a listing, foreign companies must undertake extensive SEC filings and generally provide financial reporting similar to that of U.S. companies. This helps U.S. holders weigh performance results against domestic investment alternatives.

The ADR Market

Foreign companies issuing ADRs include household names like Sony and British Airways. Investors looking for smaller companies also will find stocks like Kuala Lumpur Kepong, a Malaysian plantation group.

Privatization programs in the world's developing nations are spawning large companies with voracious appetites for international capital and recognition. For rapidly growing companies, ADRs are an effective form of advertising and fund raising. The receipts may be used to establish a trading record, gain a following among investors and securities analysts, and pave the way for raising U.S. capital in the future.

As a publicly traded security in the U.S., an ADR may be used for cross-border mergers and acquisitions. The British jeweler Ratners, for example, used a convertible preferred ADR stock swap to acquire Kay Jewelers, a major U.S. jewelry chain.

The increasing need for foreign companies to gain access to international capital markets will increase the liquidity of ADRs and make more companies available for investing in ADR form. The greater the liquidity, the greater the opportunities for investors on the international scene—including, of course, value investors.

An ADR Success Story

The story of Compañía de Telefónos de Chile (CTC) offers an illustration of how and why foreign-domiciled companies issue ADRs.

CTC, which owns 94 percent of all phone lines in Chile, could not raise the necessary funds at home to ease the country's phone service shortfall. The objective, according to Claudio Garcia, CTC's senior executive vice president of finance and administration, was to triple service by 1996. Garcia determined it would take $1.7 billion to achieve that goal.

At the time of CTC's planned expansion, the capitalization of Chile's entire stock market was just $11.6 billion, or barely one-fourth the value of AT&T's outstanding stock. Trading hours for the Santiago exchange were limited to an hour and a half each day, and average daily trading volume was only 3.9 million shares.

CTC needed access to greater capital flows. In 1990, the company took the unprecedented step of using an ADR as a new-stock issue. CTC's U.S. offering was the first by a Latin American company in 27 years.

CTC was granted a direct NYSE listing, and its ADR was priced at $15.125, raising $100 million for the company. CTC's domestic bankers and suppliers were duly impressed when the ADR attracted four times as many subscribers as it could handle.

Prior to its U.S. offering, CTC was legally off limits for Chile's private pension fund investors. The country's pension managers are barred by law from investing in any company in which a single investor owns 45 percent or more, and Spain's Telefónica de España controlled nearly 50 percent of CTC. The U.S. offering diluted Telefónica's interest to 43 percent, which gave CTC future access to Chile's lucrative pension funds.

Disadvantages of ADR Investing

Despite their many benefits to issuers and investors alike, ADRs also have the following potential drawbacks:

1. Additional costs may be incurred in creating or canceling ADRs, and these costs could be passed on to the investor.

2. The ADR-issuing bank may keep a portion of the dividend as payment for services. (That is a negative, of course, but the bank is also performing a major currency exchange transaction that converts the dividend payment from the company's local currency to U.S. dollars. The bank transaction reduces exchange costs dramatically for the single investor.)

3. ADRs are usually not available for small companies in the early stages of their existence. Most companies that have ADR listings are already mature entities.

4. Lack of disclosure for OTC-listed ADRs. Some companies choose not to list their ADRs on U.S. exchanges. Listing is mandatory for any foreign company that seeks to raise capital in the U.S., but not every firm is seeking money from American investors. Since there are costs involved in meeting the accounting and reporting requirements of the SEC, a nondomestic company may not want to go through the expense of producing an ADR.

On Borrowed Time?

The pros and cons of buying ADRs could become a moot point if, as some investors believe, ADRs disappear from the market altogether. The jury is still out as to whether and when this might happen.

Some international market watchers foresee a brilliant but brief future for ADRs. They figure that once the world's exchanges become electronically integrated, the role of ADRs will diminish considerably. Thanks to computers and telecommunications, everyone in the world will be buying the same ordinary shares through electronic means.

Dematerialization, or the replacement of physically delivered certificates with electronic record keeping, has already occurred in many of the world's exchanges. Fixed commissions are also disappearing from many major markets. And competition among ADR custodial banks is pulling down processing fees.

ORDINARIES

Another way to invest in a foreign company is to buy its shares—also known as ordinaries—directly on its home exchange. Here is what happens when an individual investor opts for direct purchase of ordinaries:

1. The investor chooses a nondomestic company that he or she would like to own.
2. The investor gets in touch with a local stockbroker.
3. The broker goes into the over-the-counter market to find a major institutional foreign stockbroker.
4. The institutional foreign broker places the order in the stock's country of origin and buys the shares in the currency of that country.
5. The institutional foreign broker exchanges the foreign currency for dollars, marks up the investment, and sells it to the U.S. broker.
6. The U.S. broker serves as custodian for the shares.

Virtually every major domestic brokerage firm can purchase ordinary shares of foreign companies, even if the brokerage does not have an office in the foreign country-of-origin for those particular shares.

Keeping Markups Manageable

The markup charged by foreign brokers typically ranges from 25 to 50 basis points (0.25 percent to 0.50 percent). That is a negligible number over time—assuming you are willing to be a long-term owner of foreign stocks. And if you are a value investor, by definition you are an owner, not a trader. That is true whether you are buying Siemens ordinaries or AT&T common.

It is a different (and more expensive) story, however, if you are a trader who constantly buys and sells stocks in search of the quick hit. Those with short time horizons find that transaction costs add up quickly overseas, and most traders are better off dealing with a broker who has offices in the company's home country.

U.S. Broker as Custodian of Foreign Shares

American investors are often surprised to learn that their local brokerage house can custody ordinary shares. As custodian, your stateside broker is responsible for paying out dividends in U.S. dollars.

Typically, the domestic brokerage would have a sub-custodial relationship with a foreign bank. If, for example, you were to buy Dutch ordinaries, the foreign broker would deliver those shares to a Dutch bank that has a custodial relationship with your U.S. broker. Thereafter, the foreign shares would show up on your regular monthly statement, along with your U.S. shares.

Once purchased, ordinaries may be held in the same electronic depository as U.S. shares. The U.S. electronic depository system is expanding its influence in foreign markets, which simplifies the process of buying ordinary shares.

Ratio of Ordinaries to ADRs

Some ADRs represent underlying shares or ordinaries on a one-for-one basis. For example, one ordinary share in the Italian Benetton Group equals one ADR. Other ADRs represent more or less than one underlying share. Ten ordinaries of British Telecom, for example, equals one ADR. On the other hand, it takes a mere 0.01 underlying share of Swiss-based Nestle to equal one ADR.

The number of ordinaries represented by a single ADR reflects the overall pricing of shares on a national stock market. In Hong Kong, where quoted prices for blue-chip companies are often under $1 per share, an ADR usually represents multiple shares.

In Switzerland, the quoted price is often more than $1,000 per blue-chip-company share. While the Hong Kong market welcomes small-investor participation, the Swiss market almost exclusively targets large-scale or institutional buyers.

Hong Kong's small-user-friendly pricing and stock splits reflect this focus on the individual investor. In Switzerland, a land of sky-high stock quotes and precious few stock splits, the single investor is understandably a rare bird.

From the standpoint of investment value, these pricing policies are meaningless. Comparing a Hong Kong share that sells for $1 with a Swiss share that sells for $1,000 tells you nothing about the underlying worth of the companies in question.

Stock splits is another red herring that tends to confuse the investing public. Although splitting a stock has no impact on the value of a business, investors often view the announcement as positive news. Any short-term buying blip that follows the announcement should be looked upon as speculating rather than investing. From where we sit, stock splits are a minor annoyance that drive up the price of liquidating shares.

ADRs vs. Ordinaries

Oftentimes you have a choice between buying a foreign company's ADR and its ordinary shares. Assuming the company meets the value criteria we have discussed, what is the best way to invest?

In comparing the relative merits of ADRs and direct purchase of ordinary foreign shares, investors should consider each of the following factors.

Pricing

In theory, ADRs are slightly more expensive than underlying ordinaries, since ADR prices include holding charges, processing costs, and the market maker's spread. However, large price differences between ADRs and underlying shares are quickly eliminated by arbitrageurs. Sometimes the use of a single domestic broker in ADR trading actually winds up costing less than purchasing ordinaries with a non-U.S. brokerage firm. And non-U.S. investors sometimes buy ADRs to obtain lower commissions and avoid stamp taxes.

Arbitrageurs are professional investors who buy a security in one market and sell it in another to exploit momentary pricing differentials. Typically, arbitrageurs employ huge leverage to turn small pricing differences into substantial profits. Since arbitrageurs are often brokers or banks, they generally have a lower brokerage cost threshold and a lower fund cost to overcome than does the general public. Given their position in the marketplace, arbitrageurs can make a profit by exploiting the minute price differences between ADRs and ordinaries.

Settlement Time

Trades in ordinaries can take up to three months to settle, while the required settlement time for ADRs is three days. This is a particularly important difference for major institutional investors who must regularly report to their customers. Trades that remain unsettled for long periods of time within a pension fund are intolerable for the corporate treasurer in charge of the fund. The long-term cost for this individual could be a diminished professional reputation or even, in some cases, the loss of his or her job.

Even for the independent investor, a lengthy settlement period can be unnerving. After all, who wants to pay for a security and then wait several months to receive it?

Convenience

Buying ADRs avoids the headaches of dealing directly in the overseas market. You deal with your regular broker, who charges you their standard commission to buy the ADR on an exchange or over-the-counter. Receipts are issued by American banks, which take physical possession of the foreign securities and are responsible for converting dividends into dollars and deducting foreign withholding taxes for you.

Language barriers are nonexistent, since annual reports and other shareholder correspondence are printed in English. This allows you to readily compare ADR holdings with domestic investment alternatives. And you don't have to contend with a multitude of time zones and currency conversions.

The collection of dividends on ordinaries can be a confusing process, since regulations differ from country to country. In Japan, for instance, the investor must present certificates of ownership to the firm or agent prior to receiving dividends.

Access to Information

Typically, ADRs have a better information flow than ordinary shares and eliminate the need for costly international communications. Companies with ADRs that trade on U.S.-listed exchanges must file a 20-F report with the Securities and Exchange Commission on an annual basis, which is comparable to the Form 10-K required of U.S. companies.

The 20-F includes a balance sheet, profit and loss statement, and statement of cash flow. In some cases, a cash-flow statement may not even be required in the company's home market. This in-depth reporting of total sales, revenue, pretax operating income, and sales according to separate classes of products and business lines is thereafter regarded as public information.

Even companies with nonlisted ADRs usually publish an English-language version of their annual report. Foreign companies with no ADRs may not go to the expense of producing financial reports in English.

Frequently, a foreign company with ADRs trading in the U.S. hires an investor relations firm to provide information on an as-needed basis. The PR firm may even sponsor conference calls between investors and company management. Each January, for instance, the investor-relations arm of Elf Aquitaine sets up a conference call in which investors are able to talk to the company's chairman about the previous year's results and expectations for the upcoming year.

Liquidity

A common misconception about ADRs is that they provide insufficient liquidity, particularly for large institutional investors. Some U.S. fund managers contend that they have to buy ordinaries because the ADR market does not have sufficient transaction volume to support major buy and sell orders.

This is simply not true. Arbitrageurs will always provide the needed liquidity and convert ADRs into their underlying ordinaries. And all ADRs—whether sponsored, unsponsored, exchange-listed, or OTC-traded—are immediately convertible into ordinary shares. At most, you are looking at an extra day or so to achieve the conversion.

If you are more of a gunslinger than a serious owner and want to get in and out of the market fast, you might insist on the hour-by-hour liquidity that ordinaries provide. Otherwise, what's the hurry? If you are a patient, value-oriented investor, you will be more concerned with tracking long-term business trends than responding to short-term, irrational blips in the price of a foreign stock.

Price Quotes

Getting a quote on an exchange-listed ADR is easy. Simply look on the NASDAQ, NYSE, and other U.S. market pages of *The Wall Street Journal* or the business section of your local newspaper.

Finding prices for unlisted ADRs that trade over-the-counter is tougher. (Roughly three-quarters of ADRs trade in the OTC market.) You can call your stockbroker for an instant quotation, or you could consult the Foreign Markets section of *The Journal* for the approximate market value of an ordinary stock. Here, however, prices are quoted in their domestic currency, so you are not finished. To convert the value of your stock to U.S. dollars, find *The Journal's* listing of currency exchange rates. Then multiply the foreign stock quote by the U.S. currency rate.

Keep in mind that in some cases one ADR does not equal one ordinary share. If, for example, one of your ADR holdings represents five ordinaries, multiply the quoted value of the foreign stock, times the US. currency rate, times 5 to obtain the current value of your ADR.

PACKAGED OVERSEAS INVESTMENTS

Unless you have the time and inclination to research foreign companies, you might want to bypass ADRs and ordinaries in favor of prepackaged overseas investments such as mutual funds. The latter fall into four broad categories: (1) global funds, which invest in all countries, including the U.S.; (2) international funds, which invest in all countries except the U.S.; (3) regional funds, which invest in particular areas of the world such as Europe or Asia or Latin America; and (4) single-country funds, which invest in one particular country, such as Mexico or France.

Open- vs. Closed-End Funds

After choosing between global, international, regional, and single-country funds, there is still one more decision to be made. Aside from where a fund invests, there are two types of fund structures, known as open-end and closed-end.

When you invest money in an open-end fund, you receive units or shares. The open-end fund or investment company will always repurchase your shares at the net asset value (NAV) of the portfolio. Open-end funds have no set number of outstanding shares; as more money comes in, the fund issues more shares (at the net asset value) and the fund manager buys more securities with the new money.

A closed-end fund is both a company and a fund, with a fixed number of outstanding shares that trade either on an exchange or over-the-counter. The value of the shares is set by the market. Although the share price is closely related to the value of the fund's underlying net assets, often there is a deviation between these two figures. Shares of a closed-end fund can trade at either a discount from the underlying value (NAV) of the stocks in the fund, or at a premium.

Two good sources of information on closed-end funds are *Barron's*, whose weekly listing includes the amount of each fund's current discount or premium to net asset value, and *The Wall Street Journal*. Also consider *Morningstar Mutual Funds*, which includes detailed individual summaries of both open- and closed-end funds.

Before diving into the fund selection process, there are a few terms that you should understand.

Net Asset Value (NAV)

A fund's NAV is the market value of its holdings (after deducting liabilities) divided by the number of shares outstanding. When you consult the mutual-fund listings in your daily newspaper, the NAV appears in the first column after the name of the fund and represents the price at which the holder can sell a share of the fund.

Loads

Also known as sales charges, loads are applied in one of two ways. Some funds impose front-end loads, in which the sales charge is deducted from the amount going to buy shares. For example, a fund with a 4.5 percent front-end load would deduct $45 for every $1,000 invested. Back-end loaded funds access a deferred sales charge, with the amount of the load dependent on the length of time the shares were held. A typical back-end-loaded fund would impose a 5 percent sales fee on shares sold within the first year after purchase, 4 percent on sales within the second year, and so on until liquidations made after year five are free. Funds that don't impose a front- or back-end load are known as no-load funds.

Operating Expenses

Day-to-day expenses are passed along to shareholders and deducted directly from fund earnings. The amount of a fund's operating costs varies according to the type of asset being managed and where the fund operates. For example, stock funds with all or a portion of their holdings invested overseas usually have the highest expenses, typically around 1.8 percent of average annual net assets. Domestic stock funds have expense ratios around 1.4 percent, while operating costs for bond offerings are usually below 1 percent per year. Published track records for mutual funds are after deducting operating expenses.

Value Tips on Choosing a Fund

As a value investor, a good bet is to buy discounted closed-end regional and single-country funds. Often, discounts can reach 15 percent or more, particularly when global sentiment about a market or region becomes unfavorable.

In general, however, buying an underwritten, closed-end fund at the offering price is not a good idea. Any time you buy a closed-end fund at the time of the initial under-writing, you are paying a premium to cover the costs of the underwriting.

There are important exceptions, however, such as in the case of the Brazil Fund in 1991 and 1992. The Brazilian equity market at that time was essentially closed to foreign investors, and the only viable means of participation was through the closed-end Brazil Fund. But when a market is trading at a mere three times earnings (as Brazil was during those years), value investors could decide that paying a small premium is acceptable if the closed-end fund is the only viable means for investing in a market that offers compelling value.

International Private Investment Management

For individuals with substantial assets, international private investment management could be just the ticket. While the vast majority of international money managers have multi-million-dollar minimum account sizes, some are willing to settle for smaller account minimums.

Finding the Right Manager

In a nation with thousands of registered investment advisors, finding a qualified manager who meets your particular needs can be a daunting task. One option is to ask for a recommendation from your local stockbroker. Most of the nation's major brokerage firms now offer investment man-agement consulting services and maintain databases that cover many of the top investment managers. This informa-tion includes a manager's track record, personnel, philoso-phy, investment style, and fees.

Setting Your Objectives

The first step in finding an investment manager is to understand your own investment goals. If you are on the verge of retirement, preservation of capital might be high on your list of objectives. If you are a young executive on the move, growth of capital might take precedence.

An astute consultant will make sure that you understand the long-term risk-and-reward characteristics of stocks, bonds, and cash equivalents. Obviously, not everyone has the same tolerance for risk. If gambling 10 percent of your nest egg to earn a 20 percent return would give you chronic insomnia, then you should look for a more conservative investment strategy.

Based on your personal investment goals and risk profile, your financial consultant will recommend one or more managers whose philosophy and investing style mesh comfortably with your own.

Consultants Perform Due Diligence

Reputable investment consultants routinely send out teams of analysts to monitor investment management firms. Good performance, of course, is part of the picture, but more important are the quality of the portfolio manager's professional staff, the consistency of the manager's investment strategy, and the nature of the strategy itself.

Consultants are forever on the lookout for red flags, such as a sudden shift in investment style, the perils of runaway growth, or changes in key personnel. For example, a value-style investment manager who starts chasing growth stocks because that sector happens to be hot at a given moment is not doing what he or she was hired to do. And sometimes firms can become victims of their own success, taking on too many clients too quickly and losing control of the quality of their product.

Common Sense

In the last two chapters, we have explained why diversifying your portfolio to include a healthy sampling of foreign stocks makes good old common sense. We also have talked about how to get involved, including everything from ADRs to ordinaries to mutual funds to professional investment management.

Regardless of how you choose to invest overseas, however, there are certain aspects that are unique to the process. These will be described in Chapter 10.

10

C H A P T E R

Unique Aspects of Foreign Investing

There is little doubt that adding a sprinkle of carefully selected foreign holdings can add return to a portfolio while lowering its risk. The previous two chapters described the unique benefits of international investing, as well as how to decide on the proper amount and means of buying foreign securities.

It is important to keep in mind, however, that along with the likelihood of enhanced return and diminished volatility over time, comes a unique set of factors. These factors are the result of currency fluctuations, differences in accounting practices, and vastly different political environments.

Following are explanations of each of these unique factors of international investing.

CURRENCY FLUCTUATION

Changes in currency exchange rates are a double-edged sword. Sometimes, fluctuations in the exchange rate between the dollar and a foreign currency can work to the disadvantage of American investors; at other times it can help.

The underlying principle, however, is actually fairly simple. All other things being equal, if the U.S. dollar rises against the currency of the country in which you are investing, the value of your ADR or foreign-denominated asset falls. For example, if the U.S. dollar rises in value against the Mexican peso, the dollar value of Mexican equity holdings will decrease. Conversely, if the dollar drops against the currency of the country in which you are investing, your foreign investment rises. When the dollar falls against the Japanese yen, for example, the value of Japanese holdings for American investors rises.

Why Exchange Rates Fluctuate

Many factors influence the value of a country's currency. First, a currency doesn't necessarily move in simultaneous lockstep—or even in the same direction—against the monetary units of every nation. Over the last 30 years, for example, the U.S. dollar has drifted gradually lower against the Japanese yen and German mark, but has mostly climbed against the majority of the world's other currencies.

Second, the price of a nation's currency relative to another is set by supply and demand, just like the values for other asset classes. When the economy in one nation is growing strongly and without significant inflation, its financial assets become attractive to global investors, who in turn buy the currency in order to pay for the stocks or bonds. Other flow-of-funds considerations are important as well, such as a country's balance of trade. The major factor exerting downward pressure on the dollar versus the yen has been the large trade surplus Japan has enjoyed over the United States in recent years. The net effect of the trade imbalance between the two countries is to cause the selling of dollars and the buying of yen.

Finally, currencies experience bull and bear phases just like stocks and bonds. Since the Federal Reserve Board established its trade-weighted dollar index in the early 1970s, the American greenback has experienced more than a dozen moves of 15 percent or more in either direction. Similar short-term cycles occur between the currencies of individual nations. Just as with other financial assets, however, price trends in the foreign-exchange market eventually reverse. Over the long haul, changes in the relative values of currencies are often small and unpredictable.

Hedging and the Value Investor

One way to deal with the potential impact of changes in international exchange rates is through a strategy called hedging. Used primarily by institutional investors, hedging involves buying derivatives contracts (usually futures or options) to lock in a predetermined rate of exchange between the dollar and the currency of whatever country in which investments are contemplated.

Though the strategy appears attractive, it is important to remember that as hedging decreases risk, it also decreases return on investment. For hedging to be effective, both the amount and duration of the investment should be known. Hedging is not recommended for the value investor, since it is impossible to predict when an undervalued stock will reach its fair value, a process that may take anywhere from a few months to five years.

Foreign exchange markets are short-term oriented and not equipped to handle contracts that could last for five years. On average, foreign exchange futures contracts represent $80,000, and options contracts represent $40,000. Unless an investor has at least this amount of currency exposure, it is impossible to create a perfect hedge.

A well-diversified international portfolio rarely will have more than a 10 percent exposure to any one country. At that allocation level, currency hedging would reduce the total fund risk by a mere 0.0006 percent. Consequently, currency hedging is attractive only if the associated costs are low. Unfortunately, hedging can be a very costly procedure. Hedging costs include brokerage commissions and bid-asked spreads. The contracts also have to be rolled over every six months or so, incurring the same costs each time. And the premium on a derivatives contract can run anywhere from 2 percent to 7 percent, cutting deeply into any potential returns on the stock.

Another important factor to consider is that currency fluctuation has never been a major risk component in a diversified portfolio. For example, the French stock market has a standard deviation (risk) of 21.6 percent, excluding currency exposure, and when measured with currency risk, there is a 25.45 percent standard deviation. This results in a currency risk that totals only 3.85 percent of the total risk. And as noted earlier, currency fluctuations tend to even out in the long run, making hedging a costly and unnecessary gamble.

On the other hand, exposure to foreign currencies acts as a diversifying tool, similar to investing in various overseas markets. For example, if the dollar depreciates (as it generally has over the last 25 years), a portfolio holding only dollar-based assets will also experience a sharp decline in world purchasing power. But if the same portfolio were internationally diversified, the effects of any dollar depreciation would be mitigated by the foreign currency exposure. This is especially beneficial to the value investor, since value opportunities are often found in countries where the currency is weak. Undervalued currencies are less likely to experience large depreciations.

POLITICAL RISK

We all have seen how quickly an ideal political scenario can sour, and vice versa. In an extreme case, political upheaval can wipe out an entire portfolio. Anyone who happened to be fully invested in Chile when Salvador Allende began nationalizing major industries in 1971 could have lost everything. But this scenario is rare and easily avoidable.

The best defense against political risk is diversification. Properly diversified international equity portfolios limit investments in a single country to 20 percent of assets. Allocations to countries that have higher risk levels should remain between 0 percent and 5 percent. By limiting exposure to any one country, only a small portion of the total portfolio can be affected by a particular political risk. In addition, the value investor is a long-term holder of a stock and is willing to endure temporary drops in a country's stock market. For example, after Tiananmen Square, Hong Kong stocks fell substantially. But the ever-patient value investor eventually saw stock prices gradually surpass their original values.

Some value investors even view political risk in a positive light, since the resulting uncertainty creates good buying opportunities. The best time to buy is after stocks have plunged and a market is selling at a relatively cheap price. Instead of viewing the Tiananmen Square massacre as a warning sign not to invest in the Hong Kong market, the value investor would take it as a sign to start accumulating shares.

When evaluating political risks, the value investor should consider the attitude of opposition political groups, the level of stability in the labor market, the country's economic sensitivity to energy costs, and the government's policies toward foreign investment and private enterprise.

DIVERSE ACCOUNTING SYSTEMS

In sports, all teams play by the same set of rules. Three strikes and you are out—whether you are a New York Yankee or a Los Angeles Dodger.

Keeping score is a lot more confusing in the international investment arena, where each country has its own set of accounting rules and corporate disclosure practices.

And even when the names are the same, they don't necessarily mean the same thing. Take the price-earnings ratio, for instance. In February 1992, Wall Street's Standard & Poor's Industrial Index was selling at 25.6 times earnings, compared with 36.7 for the Tokyo equity market. But Andrew Smithers of Smithers & Co., a London research firm, argued that Tokyo's real P/E was 20.2, or just 57 percent of the stated ratio. The reason? Roughly 45 percent of the shares on Tokyo's market were owned by another quoted company, a system known as cross-ownership. To own the entire market, Smithers reasoned, an investor would only have to buy 55 percent of the Tokyo bourse.

Confusing? You bet. But that same confusion creates opportunity to those who understand the differences in global accounting methods. In this chapter we offer general accounting guidelines for comparing equities across international borders.

The Challenge of Diversity

International accounting uniformity is an idea whose time is coming—slowly. Despite notable exceptions, the international investment arena remains a confusing world of diverse accounting practices. Any foreign company with a listing on U.S. exchanges must satisfy U.S. GAAP (generally accepted accounting principles) reporting standards. Some multinationals, such as Honda and Matsushita, fulfill this requirement by issuing two sets of accounting statements, one to meet local standards, and a second for purposes of U.S. GAAP. Other companies use a single report to publish results in accordance with their own national accounting requirements. Within the framework of that same report, numbers are converted into U.S. GAAP terms.

The challenge for international stock pickers is to compare the earnings of companies on a worldwide basis, despite national accounting discrepancies. It's a challenge we welcome as value investors, because it gives us a leg up on the competition in the hunt for bargain stocks. If uncovering the bottom-line truth about a foreign company's financial status were a quick and easy task, surface investors would do it, too.

How to Compare Apples and Oranges

In comparing the real prices of worldwide equities, here are some points to consider.

• Compare cash flows rather than reported earnings. Although cash flow per share requires adjustment for differing accounting methods, the statistic is generally more comparable than earnings.

• Comparing international book values is meaningless unless you interpret the underlying accounting principles in each case. Even under U.S. GAAP, accounting book values rarely reflect true market asset values.

• Dividends don't lie. If you are comparing a U.S. company with a nondomestic company in the same field and both have similar business fundamentals, the foreign stock paying an 8 percent dividend could be a better buy than the domestic stock paying 3 percent. Dividends are paid in hard, cold cash, leaving no room for accounting interpretations.

• Some countries—such as Switzerland, Germany and Japan—are more conservative than others when it comes to reporting earnings.

• Some overseas companies, particularly when reporting extraordinary earnings from sales of subsidiaries or real estate, may report these earnings less conservatively than they would under U.S. GAAP standards.

• Tax considerations affect the way in which non-U.S. companies report their earnings. In Germany and Switzerland, tax authorities do not permit businesses to maintain two sets of books. The shareholders and the tax authorities receive identical earnings reports. Therefore, reports to shareholders minimize earnings to avoid a heavier tax bite.

• Under U.S. GAAP, net income before taxes as reported to shareholders often differs from net income as computed on the company's tax return. A domestic company could, for instance, use one depreciation schedule for reporting to its stockholders, and a different set for reporting to the IRS. For example, suppose Company ABC buys a $100,000 piece of equipment. In reporting to stockholders, the company may opt for straight-line depreciation over a 20-year period. This approach reduces reported earnings by a mere $5,000 during that first year and in subsequent years. For tax reporting purposes, on the other hand, Company ABC may elect the double-declining-balance method of depreciation. First-year depreciation would be $10,000, which temporarily reduces the profit by an additional $5,000, as compared with the straight-line method. The result is a temporary reduction in the amount of earnings reported to the IRS, thereby reducing the tax bite.

Regardless of the method used, over the life of the asset the amount of depreciation will be the same. But by using accelerated depreciation in its reporting to the IRS, Company ABC can conserve more of its cash during the early years of an asset's useful life. And by using straight-line depreciation in its reporting to stockholders, Company ABC can present a more favorable earnings picture.

When comparing companies' results on an international basis, keep in mind that diverse depreciation methods produce diverse earnings reports. Cash flows, on the other hand, are less affected by different depreciation expenses. Therefore, in assessing corporate performance, international stock pickers should take a hard look at cash flows as well as reported earnings.

Not Better or Worse . . . Just Different

Uniformity might be easier to achieve if one set of accounting standards were demonstrably superior to all the others. As it happens, reporting rules in foreign countries are not necessarily better or worse than U.S. GAAP, they are just different. Financial accounting is a somewhat subjective process. Accountants often make assumptions about the future that understandably differ from country to country.

In the United States, reporting profit margins on product lines is viewed as standard accounting procedure. In Germany, corporations equate such disclosures with giving away important secrets to competing firms. The New York Stock Exchange has barred German companies from trading as exchange-listed ADRs unless and until these companies agree to report profit margins on a line-by-line basis.

Comparing Goodwill

Domestic firms tend to pump up book values by their method of accounting for goodwill, especially relative to their foreign-based cousins. At the end of September 1996, the stated U.S. GAAP accounting book value for Philip Morris was $17.65 per share. However, the company had $18.7 billion, or the equivalent of $23.05 per share, listed under goodwill.

Over the years, Philip Morris had acquired several leading brand names, including Kraft cheeses, Miracle Whip salad dressing, Miller beer, Sanka and Maxwell House coffees, and Post cereals. These brand names, which possess intangible economic value, were categorized as goodwill by the Philip Morris accounting staff.

Under Swiss accounting principles, the number for Philip Morris would look quite different. Instead of $17.65 book value, the company would have a negative book value of –$5.40 ($17.65 – $23.05). The Swiss do not ascribe a monetary value to goodwill.

A straight comparison between the rates of return on equity for Philip Morris and Nestle, a comparable Swiss firm, would be meaningless. The value of such companies is determined in large part by the earning power generated by their brand names, advertising, and distribution clout. An investor has to look behind the numbers and understand what accounting principles are being used. In comparing these companies, asset value analysis is, candidly, a waste of time; you need to analyze their earning power instead.

You might start by comparing the treatment of goodwill on the income statements for the two firms. In accordance with U.S. GAAP requirements, goodwill must be amortized and eventually eliminated from the balance sheet entirely by subtracting a set amount from earnings on an annual basis. Even if the Kraft name endures forever, its goodwill value for accounting purposes has a finite life span.

Swiss accounting practices handle goodwill differently. As long as chocoholics smack their lips over a Nestle's Crunch bar, the company need not write off accounting goodwill associated with the Nestle name. To translate the value of the Nestle company into U.S. accounting terms, however, goodwill amortization must be subtracted from the corporation's earnings.

Should Kraft cheeses or Nestle chocolate have a longer shelf life than the goodwill value of their product names? We don't think so. Writing off accounting goodwill for a prestigious brand name does not reflect the true economics of the situation. In our opinion, Swiss accounting is more accurate than U.S. GAAP in its treatment of trade names.

A Tale of Two Phone Companies

In 1991, Telefónica de España, Spain's major phone company, was a better buy than Pacific Telesis, a large U.S. exchange. But you wouldn't have known it from a cursory glance at the firms' accounting sheets. The stated P/E ratio for Telefónica de España in the Spanish accounting report was equivalent to the P/E ratio for Pacific Telesis in U.S. GAAP figures.

In reality, Telefónica was trading at half the price of the U.S. company, based on earnings. In 1989, the earnings per share as stated in Telefónica's annual report were $2.03. In 1990, earnings rose to $2.56, and in 1991 to $2.92. Converted to U.S. accounting, the earnings for the three years would have been $4.46, $5.50, and $5.70, respectively.

The primary reason for these discrepancies is that Spanish accounting mandates the use of relatively rapid depreciation rates for plants and equipment. Of late, these depreciation write-offs have been particularly large and reflect Telefónica's substantial investments in new plants and equipment. Under U.S. accounting codes, depreciation schedules could be extended for longer periods of time, and Telefónica's earnings would look higher.

Who Is Right and Who Is Wrong?

The Spanish accounting rationale goes something like this: By rapidly writing off very large investments in state-of-the-art phone equipment, you are acknowledging the speed of innovation in the telecommunications industry. Equipment becomes obsolete rather quickly, as new technology comes on line.

Proponents of American accounting practices might counter by saying: Rapid write-off of equipment that is not yet obsolete or even close to it does not fairly reflect business dynamics or the profitability of an expanding company.

For investors, the issue isn't which accounting method is right or wrong. Focus on understanding how different points of view affect the bottom line, in this case, domestic and non-U.S. share earnings. At the end of 1991, Telefónica was trading at 12 times earnings in Spanish accounting terms. If the earnings were translated into U.S. terms, the company would be selling at a bargain P/E ratio of 6.5.

At the same time, Pacific Telesis Group, the large California telephone company, was trading at 15.5 times earnings. Telefónica de España, therefore, was a bargain, compared to Pacific Telesis.

EXAMPLES OF COUNTRY ACCOUNTING DIFFERENCES

As you can see from the saga of the phone companies, it is easy to misjudge the value qualities of an overseas issue when you look at financial statements. The following country examples underscore some of the differences in accounting procedures.

Japan[1]

Accounting practices in Japan are so heavily influenced by tax regulations that earnings and asset values are often understated. Any item that is claimed for tax purposes must be included in the financial statements that shareholders receive.

Real Estate: Revaluation of property is not permitted. Therefore, when land prices soared in the 1980s, land assets remained at book values that were far below current market price.

Depreciation: Whereas U.S. companies employ straight-line depreciation, the Japanese use double-declining depreciation, an accelerated form of depreciation that understates fixed assets and earnings. If Japanese companies employed the straight-line method, current earnings would increase on average between 10 and 15 percent. Straight-line depreciation reduces the value of an asset in equal annual increments. Assuming no residual value, a $20,000 auto with a useful life of five years might be valued at $16,000 after one year, $12,000 after two years, and so on.

Double-declining depreciation reduces the value of an asset by greater chunks in the early years of an asset's estimated life. Depreciation on the auto during the first year would be $8,000 rather than $4,000. Thereafter, depreciation charges gradually decrease.

Earnings per share calculations: Under U.S. GAAP, the method for calculating earnings per share is consistent for all domestic companies. U.S. firms must report earnings per share and include information related to continuing operations, discontinued operations, income before extraordinary items, changes in accounting principles, and net income. These disclosures are far more comprehensive than anything required under Japanese GAAP.

Goodwill: Goodwill arising from consolidation is normally amortized over a five-year period by the Japanese, as compared with the 40 years permissible under U.S. GAAP. This understates the company's asset value compared to a similar U.S. firm.

United Kingdom[2]

In many respects, financial statements prepared in the United Kingdom are similar to those prepared according to U.S. GAAP. However, U.K. companies have a broader choice of accounting methods. The use of alternative accounting methods under U.K. accounting standards (Statements of Standard Accounting Practice, or SSAPs) opens the door to a variety of interpretations.

Goodwill: In the U.K., goodwill may be either written off immediately by charging it against shareholder's equity, or be capitalized and amortized. There is no requirement that either approach be used consistently. However, under U.S. GAAP, goodwill must be capitalized and amortized over a period of not more than 40 years.

Typically, U.K. companies write off goodwill against retained earnings at the time of acquisition. When the capitalization and amortization approach is used, the amortization period is typically shorter than that used by a U.S. firm.

Inventory: The major difference between U.K. and U.S. inventory accounting is that the LIFO (last-in, first-out) method is not permissible for tax purposes in the U.K. and is seldom used. LIFO is used by a large percentage of major U.S. firms. During periods of rising prices, a U.K. firm's reported cost of sales would be lower than it would be for a U.S.

company using LIFO, and net income would be higher for the British firm.

Germany

German tax and reporting books are one and the same. It is a system that encourages hiding earnings in order to reduce taxes paid. German firms have been known to create hidden reserves that are equal to 100 percent of fixed assets. Compared to U.S. and U.K. standards, German firms overestimate contingent liabilities and future uncertainties. By overestimating losses, German firms understate earnings by as much as 50 to 100 percent compared with U.S. GAAP. Unlike U.S. companies, German firms are not required to provide earnings per share information.

Inventory: Inventories in Germany are typically understated for tax reasons and not revalued when prices go up. Mergers and takeovers are reported on the balance sheet based on book value rather than the actual transaction price.

Depreciation: Some German companies write off as much as 75 percent of the cost of buildings during the first year. This strategy makes sense when you consider the country's high marginal corporate tax rates. Furthermore, the appropriate long-term objective of a business is to maximize cash flow rather than reported earnings.

Assets that have been aggressively written down by Germany's accountants often appreciate over a period of years on an assets-and-earning-power basis. The true worth of many German businesses may be greatly understated.

Brazil[3]

In Brazil, where galloping inflation in the recent past has rendered financial statements meaningless, restatement of accounts is used to reflect changes in price levels. This indexing practice is not a generally accepted accounting principle in the U.S.

Indexation: Permanent asset accounts—which include fixed assets, deferred charges, investments and related depreciation, depletion, amortization, and provisions for investment losses—are restated monthly by the change in the official index for Federal Treasury Bonds. The resulting net increment in asset values is credited to the income statement. Shareholders' equity accounts are restated in the same manner, and the increment is charged to the income statement.

Historically, the Treasury Bond Index has not reflected the full change in purchasing power caused by inflation. Inventories are not restated and are therefore shown at less than current replacement cost in the balance sheet. Net income or loss for the current accounting period is not restated.

All publicly traded companies must present constant supplementary financial statements that restate the primary financial statements in terms of the monthly changes in purchasing power. Companies can successfully perform in a hyperinflationary environment, provided their expectations are realistic and they rely on indexing. In some respects, it is easier to do business and perform accounting chores in an atmosphere of hyperinflation than in a situation where 8 to 18 percent inflation is unprecedented. The United States in the 1970s and early 1980s is a case in point. During these inflationary years, U.S. accounting principles, which were based on lower rates of inflation, were misleading to managers and investors.

In countries where high inflation prevails, foreign exchange rates are generally controlled by the government. If the government sets exchange levels that are not consistent with a nation's inflation rate, accounting distortions may occur in the reports of global companies doing business within that particular country.

The Netherlands[4]

Dutch accounting is more flexible than U.S. GAAP. Although Dutch Civil Code standards are similar to American standards, the former stipulates that accounting methods should be acceptable to the business community. This phrase provides considerable accounting leeway.

Asset revaluation: In Holland, fixed assets may be revalued and stated in excess of historical cost. Replacement value is recalculated based on general price indexes. When fixed assets are revalued, depreciation expense in the income statement is based on replacement value. This increased depreciation expense may not be used for tax purposes.

Clearly, the revaluation of fixed assets can significantly increase a company's reported net assets, particularly during periods of inflation. Net income will be lower under Dutch Civil Code standards than under U.S. GAAP. In the United States, only historical cost amounts may be used for depreciation purposes. This upward revaluation of assets could conceivably allow a Dutch company to borrow more than a company in the United States.

Business Combinations: Although no one method is mandatory, purchase accounting as opposed to pooling-of-interests accounting is used in almost all cases. In the purchase accounting method, once companies are merged after an acquisition, the buying company treats the acquired company as an investment. Any premium the acquiring company pays over and above fair market value of the assets is recorded as goodwill on the buyer's balance sheet.

In the pooling-of-interests accounting methods, once companies are merged after an acquisition, the balance sheets (assets and liabilities) of the two companies are added together. Reported earnings are higher under the pooling-of-interest method than under the purchase acquisition method of accounting. Under the purchase method, any earnings of the acquired company that have occurred prior to the purchase date are not reflected in the income statement.

Korea

In late 1996 and early 1997, Korean companies generally looked cheap. The value investor was confronted with either a wonderful buying opportunity or a value trap—a seeming bargain that is, in reality, a bad investment. A brokerage report at the time sounded an ominous warning: "The dustbin of Korean investing is filled with analysts' reports claiming that Company X is the cheapest company in the world. Often times the chosen measuring stick is distorted by Korea's uniquely flexible accounting standards."[5]

Some of the "unique flexibility" has to do with very different accounting standards compared to U.S. GAAP. But a portion has to do with public confidence in the integrity of the financial data itself. In this case, the analyst is faced with two goals: assessing a comparable intrinsic worth and estimating an added discount for the risk of less than fair play. Remember, there is usually a price at which even the least promising companies can provide a good margin of safety.

The automotive manufacturer Hyundai Motor Co. Ltd. provided a striking example of the need to adjust data prior to making comparisons. In Korea, as in Japan, the government provides industries a break by allowing rapid depreciation. Depreciation is tax deductible; more rapid depreciation shelters more of today's profits, increasing after-tax cash flow. This deduction also creates an added incentive for additional investments with each marginal dollar; break-even points are lowered because of depreciation's tax shield. Consequently, this tax environment will create larger cash flow and asset values, especially during periods of growth, than for comparable U.S. companies. What is the investor to do?

In adjusting depreciation, you should note the method of depreciation and the useful lives. For example, Hyundai used accelerated methods for its assets. The company also used very short useful lives of 7 to 30 years for buildings and 3 to 6 years for machinery, tools, and equipment. The

U.S. Big Three (Ford, GM, and Chrysler) use 29 to 40 years for buildings and 5 to 27 years for machinery, tools, and equipment. A restatement of Hyundai's results would essentially reduce the tax shield provided by depreciation. Earnings would rise due to lower depreciation, but cash flow would fall because higher earnings would be offset by lower depreciation.

The Korean auto companies also capitalize research and development expenditures, which are treated as expenses in the United States. The logic for capitalization is simple: Money spent on research will produce benefits in the future, and therefore listing it as an asset on the balance sheet—to be amortized down in value over time—matches the revenue generated with the outflow of resources. Accountants call this the matching principle.

U.S. accountants tend to favor the more conservative approach, realizing that many companies will want to rename such an expense an asset simply to inflate the current period's earnings. The investor simply forges ahead with another set of adjustments.

In this case, after adjustments, Hyundai still seemed remarkably cheap compared to some of the less expensive European auto stocks at the time, principally Peugeot and Renault. The analyst then was forced to determine what advantages or weaknesses might account for the differences in price. After reviewing market shares, market conditions, export opportunities, and the like, Hyundai seemed sufficiently cheap. This view was bolstered by several contrarian indicators: The government had recently offended the trade unions who were striking a Hyundai plant, and the stock price had plunged from its previous high. It appeared to be an opportunity to purchase a decent business at a point of maximum pessimism.

As a postlude, despite all this work, actually purchasing the stock would have been difficult for the ordinary investor. Korea, still xenophobic in its investment laws, limits accessibility to shares for foreign investors. At the time, even qualified institutional buyers had a tough time locating other foreign investors who would part with their shares. These barriers are, at times, frustrating. But the patient and persistent international value investor should have a double measure of success if such hard-to-analyze and hard-to-buy issues succeed.

Comparing Companies on a Worldwide Basis

As we suggested earlier in this chapter, cash flows rather than reported earnings are a good yardstick for comparing company earnings around the globe. National accounting differences tend to distort the earnings picture for various companies.

Exhibit 10-1 compares cash flow with reported earnings, relative to stock prices. Although P/E ratios vary from country to country, this variation is reduced when you look at price-to-cash-flow multiples.

Japan is a case in point. In P/E terms, Japan looks very expensive. But if comparisons are made on a cash-flow basis, the valuations look more reasonable.

Financial Accounting: An Inexact Discipline

For the value investor seeking an attractive business at an attractive price, financial statements are a vital element in the decision-making process. As we have indicated, however, financial accounting is an inexact discipline at best. Attaching hard numbers to dynamic and perpetually changing business circumstances is an all-but-impossible task.

The reams of estimates and assumptions that are part of an accountant's stock-in-trade are invariably subject to uncertainty and interpretation. You won't find a roomful of smiling clients in a CPA waiting room any more than you would in a dentist's office. Yet, accountants obviously

E X H I B I T 10–1

Earnings and Cash Flow

	Japan		United States	
Date	Price- Earnings	Price- Cash Flow	Price- Earnings	Price- Cash Flow
06/29/90	41.10	15.60	15.50	7.90
09/28/90	27.60	10.10	13.70	6.90
12/31/90	31.00	10.60	14.10	7.30
03/29/91	35.20	11.80	16.80	8.40
06/28/91	35.00	10.90	17.50	8.40
09/30/91	36.40	10.90	18.80	8.90
12/31/91	35.30	9.90	21.70	9.90
03/31/92	29.30	8.70	24.30	10.20
06/30/92	30.20	8.20	23.60	10.10
09/30/92	36.20	8.10	23.30	10.20
12/31/92	38.90	8.10	22.70	10.20
03/31/93	43.80	9.10	23.80	10.50
06/30/93	60.70	9.80	22.50	10.00
09/30/93	71.80	10.40	21.70	9.90
12/31/93	67.80	9.80	22.10	10.40
03/31/94	74.20	10.70	19.70	9.70
06/30/94	93.70	12.10	18.80	9.50
09/30/94	88.80	11.50	18.80	9.70
12/30/94	97.30	11.60	16.90	9.10
03/31/95	80.70	9.90	16.40	9.10
06/30/95	92.20	9.90	16.90	9.60
09/29/95	123.40	12.30	17.00	9.70
12/29/95	105.20	12.90	17.20	10.00
03/29/96	107.60	13.50	17.50	10.20
06/28/96	117.43	12.77	17.77	10.42
09/30/96	100.66	12.34	18.19	10.61
12/31/96	108.69	12.13	19.34	11.18
03/31/97	94.00	11.74	19.04	11.33

display a great sense of humor when they attempt to report asset values and earnings down to the last dollar!

In addition to being humorists, some accountants seem to be in the beauty makeover business. As investors, we must be wary of accounting techniques that massage corporate results to make them look better. These practices, while strictly legal, can confound readers of financial statements. Watch out for sticky wickets such as flexible depreciation rules, off-balance-sheet financing, accounting for currency movements, treatment of costs and when to recognize them, acquisition and disposal accounting, and treatment of goodwill.

Accounting for Growth,[6] a book on "creative" British accounting, produced shock waves in the investment community. The author's conclusion—that investors should shun companies that frequently resort to "creative" accounting—is probably well taken. Companies that use liberal accounting gimmicks to hide their weaknesses are more likely than conservatively managed enterprises to spring unwelcome performance surprises in the future. Value investors beware: These accounting sleights-of-hand raise troubling questions as to management's truthfulness, its grasp on reality, and its long-term concern for shareholder interests.

And don't assume that "creative" accounting techniques are the exclusive province of foreign companies. *Unaccountable Accounting,*[7] a popular and enlightening expose on "creative" U.S. accounting techniques by Professor Abraham J. Briloff, suggests that American managers are no slouches either when it comes to "positioning" the truth.

Long-Run Reporting Smoothes Out the Bumps

Over the long term, disparities in financial reporting, caused either by "creative" accounting or by accounting standards that differ from country to country, tend to disappear. Reported foreign earnings that are higher one year than they would be under U.S. GAAP tend to be lower in a subsequent year under those same foreign accounting standards.

Value investors, whose decision making depends on basic business worth analysis, should keep in mind that one-year results are essentially meaningless. This is true not only in terms of market prices, but also as far as evaluating the intrinsic worth of businesses.

NOTES

1. Gary S. Schieneman, *Understanding Japanese Financial Statements: A Guide for the U.S. Investor* (New York: Arthur Young and Co. for Morgan Stanley, 1986).
2. Gary S. Schieneman, *Understanding U.K. Financial Statements: A Guide for the U.S. Investor* (New York: Arthur Young & Co. for Morgan Stanley, 1987).
3. Gary S. Schieneman, *Brazilian Accounting Practices and Principles* (New York: Arthur Young & Co. for Morgan Stanley, 1986).
4. Gary S. Schieneman, *Understanding Dutch Financial Statements: A Guide for the U.S. Investor* (New York: Arthur Young & Co. for Morgan Stanley, 1986).
5. Matt Cleary, *Korea: Sector Comment* (Seoul: HG Asia, January 6, 1987).
6. Terry Smith, *Accounting for Growth* (Pomfret, VT: Trafalgar Square, 1992).
7. Abraham J. Briloff, *Unaccountable Accounting* (New York: Harper & Row, 1972).

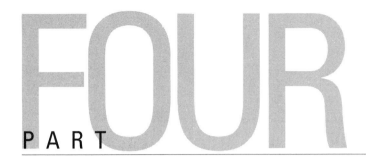

PART FOUR

VALUE INVESTING AND YOU

11

CHAPTER

Structuring Your
Value Portfolio

Superb value portfolios don't happen by accident. They are the result of careful planning and corporate sleuthing, of knowing what questions to ask, and of not being satisfied with anything less than the right answers.

But even the best plans cannot completely eliminate risk in a portfolio. In this chapter, we consider the concept of risk as it applies to value investing and explore the idea of *effective* diversification as a way to minimize risk. Arguments are presented in favor of an all-stock portfolio, with empirical evidence used to bolster this theory. Reasons why the concepts of liquidity and dollar-cost averaging do not play important roles for value investors are emphasized. Finally, since value investors will not always have their funds fully committed, several financial mechanisms have been suggested as places to park investable money.

RISK APPLIED TO VALUE INVESTING

The traditional Wall Street definition of risk involves measuring share price fluctuation. The value investor would find this approach to be unacceptable. Value investors do not lose money just because share prices decline, even if prices temporarily drop under the original cost.

Risk, for the average value investor, should be defined as the product of one of three events: loss realized through actual sale; significant deterioration in a company's position; or, more frequently, payment of more than the intrinsic worth of the security.

NOTHING LIKE DIVERSIFICATION

Risk exists even in a correctly structured value portfolio. As a result, diversification plays a strong role in lowering risk. Even with value stocks, nuggets of gold may turn out to be "fool's gold."

Purchasing only one value issue, or investing in only one industry, implies the certainty that the choice will outperform all others. That is a gamble, and while it may prove correct, the average investor is taking an unnecessary risk. Diversification—the concept of not putting all your eggs in one basket—can save you a good deal of trouble down the road. Exhibit 11-1 illustrates the beneficial impact of diversification. Notice how quickly risk declines when the number of stocks in a portfolio increases to a minimum of 20.

Given the data, should a value investor consider 20 stocks to be the limit? No. Many of the top-performing value portfolios contain hundreds of stocks. In fact, there is no level at which diversification necessarily becomes counterproductive. The main point that a value investor should keep in mind is this: *Returns are not diluted by an increased number of portfolio issues—so long as strict value criteria are followed.*

E X H I B I T   1 1 - 1

How Diversification Lowers Risk

Number of Issues in Portfolio	Percent of Total Risk	Percent by Which Risk Reduced	Cumulative Risk Reduction
1	100	0	0
2	80	20	20
3	75	5	25
4	70	5	30
5	65	5	35
6	60	5	40
7	58	2	42
8	56	2	44
9	54	2	46
10	52	2	48
15	47	5	53
20	45	2	55

Source: Peter D Heerwagen, *Investing for Total Return* (Chicago: Probus, 1988), p. 32.

Getting the Right Slant on Diversification

Benjamin Graham's arguments over diversification favored investors dividing funds between high-grade bonds and high-grade common stocks.[1] Many of today's professional investors concur in varying degrees with Graham's ideas, although my beliefs differ. Times and conditions have changed. Graham's rule was simple, mechanistic, and perhaps not appropriate for the current investing world.

Given today's investing climate, value investors should consider placing their emphasis on equities *to the total exclusion of preferred stocks or bonds.* In other words, the average value investor ideally should place 100 percent of total investable funds in diversified equities that trade at 60 percent of intrinsic value.

This is a somewhat heretical philosophy to be sure, but historical evidence is unambiguous in its conclusion: stocks outperform bonds over the long term.

Consider the results of a study by Meir Statman and Neal L. Ushman of Santa Clara University (Exhibit 11-2). Based on data gathered from 1946 to 1985, the researchers discovered that during that 40-year period a portfolio of stocks only was better than either a market portfolio (a combination of stocks and bonds) or a strictly bond portfolio.[2] Additional evidence for the long-term superiority of stocks as an asset class is provided in Chapter 12.

To be sure, full investment in equities may not always be possible. A complete complement of bargain issues occurs only about once every four or five years. Moreover, it usually takes three years from the time solid value stocks become available until sales become significant. But value investors can reasonably expect to find enough issues to be at least 25 percent invested at all times, especially if horizons have been broadened to include global issues.

When Should Stocks Be Purchased?

This is the 64-million-dollar question for many investors. The reason the answer is often so confusing is that basing buy and

EXHIBIT 11-2

Portfolios over the 1946–1985 Period

	Mean Quarterly Excess Return	Standard Deviation of Excess Return
Stocks only	1.834	7.543
Corporate bonds only	0.0060	4.653
Market portfolio	− 0.102	4.548

sell decisions on a reliable macroeconomic or top-down market view is impossible and self-defeating.

Rather than guessing where the market or the economy may be headed, here is a little rhyme to help you remember a better way to decide when to buy stocks:

> *When stocks can be found at cheap prices,*
> *the time is ripe to buy.*
> *When appropriate values cannot be found,*
> *the market is too high.*

At several points during the last 30 years—most notably 1970, 1974, 1981, 1987, and 1990—vast numbers of stocks were available at value prices; it was obvious the market was low. But the average value investor buys selected businesses, not "the market" as a whole. As such, the value investor invests according to how the market is, not where it *will* be.

Effective Diversification

Thus far the discussion has centered on an investor's portfolio mix and the number of stocks to be included. That is general diversification. The focus now can be narrowed to include only effective diversification.

Unpopular issues (read: value stocks) often are concentrated in industry sectors. The investor discovering a value stock in one particular industry should avoid other companies within the same sector. One rule of thumb to follow: no more than 20 percent of an investor's portfolio should come from one industry.

For example, a portfolio of 10 consumer electronics stocks would not be effective diversification—even if all 10 companies qualified as value stocks. Although each company would have some unique characteristics, strong group influences exist that would tend to move the stocks at the same time. Effective diversification requires stocks to be independent of each other.

Full Scientific Approach Unnecessary

A fully scientific approach to diversification requires an enormous amount of number crunching and many long hours sorting out the relationships between stocks and stock groups. And there are investment professionals who do just that, wringing out the last drop of risk reduction.

Value investors need mainly to use a little common sense to decide on an appropriate number of stocks, and then spread them over a broad spectrum of dissimilar industries.

Diversification Is Not Free

Naturally, diversification costs more—in terms of commissions, spreads, and taxes. Commissions on 200 shares each of two stocks, for example, cost more than commissions for 400 shares of a single stock. By not diversifying, however, the investor has placed an inappropriate reliance on skill (or luck) to determine investment results. Paying slightly more up front to lower your risk is well worth the cost over the long term.

Factors in Performance Evaluation

Let's assume that you have put together a portfolio of carefully selected value securities. How do you know if your stocks are performing well?

You won't know by looking at short-run results. Gains or losses over the short term should be taken with several grains of salt—or ignored altogether. Short-run performance involves randomly generated numbers; it is only a snapshot of prices, as opposed to a time exposure.

The following should be chiseled in concrete: *Don't attempt to gauge results until a portfolio has turned over at least once.* That process could take as long as three to five years. Over the short and intermediate term, the value investor should focus on whether ongoing operations match the guiding philosophy of the investment plan. If not, any gains or losses become irrelevant. Portfolios that are allowed to sail along without a well-defined plan eventually end up on the financial rocks.

Other practical lessons also surface. First, stock and/or group risk estimates are based on past behavior and are problematical at best. Moreover, relationships frequently change between the market's reaction and a specific stock or portfolio. Even past performance is not a reliable indicator of future movement.

Second, one skillful and/or lucky decision can make or break a portfolio. How would returns have appeared with Microsoft tucked snugly away from inception? And what are the chances of finding another young company with as much potential?

Consider the large returns received by a certain well-diversified partnership after it purchased 50 percent of the equity of one business. Prior to the purchase, the partnership had performed well—20 percent annually—by acquiring hundreds of value stocks. Benjamin Graham wrote of the partnership's success, "ironically enough, the aggregate of profits accruing from this single investment decision far exceeded the sum of all others realized through 20 years of wide ranging operations." Although disguised by Graham, the partnership in question was the Graham-Newman Corporation; the company was GEICO Insurance.[3]

Finally, keep in mind that performance numbers can vary enormously depending on starting and ending dates. Superb performance might become quite ordinary, and vice versa, simply by adding or subtracting one year.

LIQUIDITY

Wall Street focuses its attention largely on a stock's liquidity, i.e., the extent to which a market absorbs purchases or sales without large price changes. The reasoning is that if a problem develops in a certain company, the door is big enough for everyone to get through at the same time.

But worrying about liquidity wastes time and limits opportunity. Value investors buy good undervalued businesses and hold them for the long term. The following case illustrates how allowing liquidity concerns to impede an investment decision can lead to a costly oversight.

Delaware Trust Company, a small bank, was just one of many companies that Wall Street consistently overlooked, perhaps because analysts considered the stock to be illiquid. Yet, the company was clearly undervalued. The book value for Delaware was over $120 per share and the stock—priced at $45, when it traded—was selling at only four times earnings. After investigating every aspect of the company's financial health, I acquired a few hundred shares of Delaware stock over a six-month period. Delaware Trust traded "by appointment only," sometimes not trading for three months at a time. Every six months the bank's business activities were reviewed. Note from Exhibit 11-3 that for the first few years, very little progress was made. In 1984, however, the stock began to move dramatically.

Delaware Trust Company was purchased in 1987 by Meridien Bank, which paid shareholders $853 per share. In my case, that translated into a *33 percent annualized rate of return.* Clearly, liquidity is not important for long-term value investors. It is important only for short-term speculators.

Dollar Averaging

Proponents of a strategy known as dollar-cost averaging believe that as long as an investor can take advantage of fluctuations—buying more stock when prices fall and less when prices rise—the investor will come out all right over time.

In effect, investors using dollar-cost averaging admit they don't know what price to pay for a stock or asset. And

EXHIBIT 11-3

History of a Value Investment

As of End of February	Value of 82 shares ($)
1979	4,600
1980	5,002
1981	5,412
1982	6,437
1983	7,544
1984	10,455
1985	16,400
1986	21,320
1987	38,950
1987 (May)	70,000*

*Buyout

Relevant statistics:

On September 8, 1978, 82 shares of Delaware Trust Co. were purchased for one account for $4,600. A medium-sized, full-service bank, Delaware had $500 million in total assets in 1978. Its P/E was 4.0; price to book value 35 percent; return on equity, 8 percent; return on assets, 0.5 percent; and actual loan loss, 15 percent of reserves.

perhaps money can be made in this way, but the strategy certainly doesn't qualify as value investing.

Value investors buy when the price is right, period. Naturally, a value investor would increase a position if the stock price of a good value company declined. But value investors don't sell just because the price declines, assuming the underlying business fundamentals remain unchanged. In fact, value investors are usually interested in purchasing more stock under those circumstances.

PLACES TO PUT NONINVESTED CASH

Suppose an investor can't find enough good values and is sitting on a pocketful of cash. Rather than overpaying for a stock, the prudent investor should keep all investable funds liquid in case a bargain suddenly appears. Following are several short-term parking lots to store cash until a good value opportunity comes along.

Money Market Funds

Money market funds invest pools of assets in short-term money market instruments and take a small percentage (usually around 50 basis points) of fund earnings as a service charge.

Some money market funds invest strictly in government securities, while other portfolios hold some combination of commercial paper, short-term repurchase agreements, CDs, bankers' acceptances (used to finance foreign trade), federal agency securities, and U.S. Treasury bills. Yields on money market funds generally float 1 or 2 percent above the inflation rate.

Treasury Bills and Notes

There are scores of different government issues, each carrying different coupon rates and maturities.

Treasury bills are short-term obligations, issued with initial maturities of 3, 6, and 12 months, and sold in minimum amounts of $10,000. A new batch of 3- and 6-month T-bills is auctioned every Monday, while new issues of one-year bills are sold every month.

Ownership is signified by a Treasury book entry rather than through the more familiar engraved certificate. Prices of new bills are set by competitive investor bidding following an offering announcement. Ask your broker or bank to handle the details of the transaction. There will be a small commission or fee.

Treasury notes mature in 1 to 10 years from the date of issue. Although the minimum denomination for T-notes is $1,000, the Treasury sometimes sets higher minimums for particular issues. Besides complete assurance as to the timely payment of principal and interest, an additional benefit of Treasury securities is that interest is exempt from state taxes.

Certificates of Deposits (CDs)

Bank certificates of deposit are an attractive place to park money, *if maturities are kept short.* Rates on CDs can be higher than for either T-bills or money market funds. The staggering of maturities (owning several CDs, each with a different maturity date) permits an investor some liquidity in case an opportunity to buy a stock at a bargain price suddenly appears.

Commercial Paper

Another possibility, particularly for large investors, would be commercial paper. Usually sold in lots of $100,000, commercial paper can be purchased for maturities that range from overnight to a year or longer. Yields are slightly higher than for comparable maturities of T-bills and T-notes. Commercial paper can be bought directly from General Motors in Detroit in minimums of $10,000.

Tax-Exempt Municipal Bonds

Finally—if your tax bracket justifies it—consider short-term tax-exempt municipal bonds. These securities, which pay interest that is exempt from federal taxes, generally are priced to provide a benefit for those investors in the 28 percent federal income tax bracket or higher.

CONCLUSION

In this chapter, we have addressed risk and how effective diversification plays an important role in reducing risk. Also, we have shown that an all-stock portfolio—provided it consists entirely of carefully selected value issues—will likely provide the highest return over time. And we have listed salient reasons why liquidity concerns and dollar-cost averaging do not play significant roles for the value investor.

One additional observation: Learning to sit quietly and do nothing is probably the greatest lesson a value investor can learn. An investor should not assume that because cash is on hand, it must be invested.

The next question goes to the heart of portfolio construction: Why should you invest in common stocks at all? For the answer, turn to Chapter 12.

NOTES

1. Graham favored an investor dividing funds between high-grade bonds and high-grade common stocks. The correct proportion, he believed, would be no less than 25 percent or more than 75 percent of funds in common stocks. A corollary to his theory called for an inverse range of between 75 percent and 25 percent of funds placed in bonds. The implication was a 50/50 split between the two major investment mediums. Following that theory, if uneven changes in asset class values raised the common stock component to 55 percent, the investor would simply sell one-eleventh of a stock component and put the proceeds into bonds. And vice-versa. But times and conditions have changed. Graham's thoughts centered on conditions in late 1971 and early 1972, a period when bond yields were more than double stock yields. Moreover, he addressed himself to all of an investor's investable funds—the portion allocated for bonds or stocks. He also dismissed the effects of time horizons rather casually and failed to show the advantages that equities enjoy over bonds over the long term.

2. Meir Statman and Neal L. Ushman, "Bonds Versus Stocks: Another Look," *Journal of Portfolio Management* (Winter 1987), pp. 33–38.

3. Benjamin Graham, *The Intelligent Investor* (New York: Harper & Row), 1973, Postscript.

12

CHAPTER

Are Stocks a Good Investment?

Our economic system faces new and difficult problems. Yet industrial economies in the past have survived and even flourished under far greater economic pressures than those now being experienced. Real estate, bonds, and other assets can maintain their value only within a viable economic system. Businesses generate the wealth that fuels that system. Many investors lose sight of the fact that asset values are interrelated. If businesses falter, many other areas will be negatively affected.

Capital has always sought safe and productive havens. The usually prudent methods of capital preservation—bank deposits, bonds, and mortgages—may lead to an inexorable loss of purchasing power. Faced with weakening confidence, puzzling inflation, and greater economic uncertainty, people in the past have flooded alternative markets like art, coins, real estate, commodities, and bonds.

This chapter presents arguments in favor of equities as an *investment*—a long-haul commitment—along with insights into the inevitable ups and downs. Comparisons are made between equities and other financial alternatives. Again, the positive effect of time on an investment portfolio is emphasized, as is the challenge of dealing effectively with inflation.

STOCKS AS AN INVESTMENT

Are stocks a good investment? If history is the ultimate judge, the answer is an overwhelming yes.

According to data from Ibbotson Associates—a Chicago-based investment consulting, software, and data products firm—common stocks (as measured by the Standard & Poor's 500 Index) averaged a compounded annual return of 12.6 percent over the 50-year period through 1996, compared to 5.3 percent for long-term government bonds and just 4.9 percent for cash equivalents (Treasury bills). And while those figures may not seem drastically different from one another, consider the ultimate difference in returns over time. An investor putting $1 into the average stock at year-end 1947 would have seen the nest egg grow to $335 by 1996; that same dollar invested in government bonds would have been worth just $12.56, or 26 times less.

Another study of equity-market returns measured Benjamin Graham's stock selection criteria over a period that ranged from 1974 to 1981.[1] A control group of NYSE-Amex securities provided a mean annual return (including dividends) of 14 percent. But an investor who used Graham's criteria (and the same stock selection universe) earned an annual return of 38 percent. Furthermore, excess returns remained even after adjustment for risk.

A second 13-year study, which included the early 1980s, used essentially the same criteria. Again, the value portfolio substantially outperformed the control portfolio of NYSE-Amex and small-firm indexes.[2] For example, an investor that had placed $10,000 in a Graham-oriented portfolio on December 31, 1970, would have seen the investment increase to $254,973 by year-end 1983. The comparable figures for the NYSE-Amex and small-firm indexes would have been just $37,296 and $101,992, respectively.

What About Bear Markets?

Just as people sometimes catch a cold or flu, economies and markets also get aches and pains from time to time. Since the end of World War II, there have been 12 bear markets, or declines of 15 percent or more. The declines took the S&P 500 Index lower by an average of 26.5 percent over 11 months (see Exhibit 12-1).

EXHIBIT 12-1

Stocks and Bear Markets

Bear Market	Life Span (Months)	Price Decline (%)	First Year Rise After Decline (%)
1946	5	26.7	7.3
1947	3	15.3	20.7
1948–49	12	20.5	42.1
1956–57	15	21.6	28.2
1961–62	6	27.9	34.1
1966	6	22.2	32.8
1968–70	18	36.1	43.5
1973–74	21	48.2	34.5
1976–78	18	19.4	11.5
1980–82	22	27.1	57.7
1987	3	33.5	21.3
1990	3	19.9	28.7
Average	**11**	**26.5**	**30.2**

But people recover from their short-term illnesses, and so do stocks. In fact, the average price rise during the first year following each of the 12 postwar bear markets was nearly 31 percent.

HARD ASSETS

The historical evidence regarding the superiority of stocks relative to other financial assets is unambiguous: Stocks outperform bonds and cash equivalents by a wide margin over the long term. But what about relative returns from hard assets? Following is a brief tour of the hard or real-asset investment universe.

Gold

We've all been taught to trust the yellow metal as a reliable inflation hedge, but take a closer look. From 1781 to 1981, gold appreciated by a mere 1.6% annually. Some inflation hedge! That is less than you could have made at your neighborhood bank. And even if you were fortunate enough to bail out at the top of the metal's spectacular bull run in 1980, your returns would still have been sub par relative to equities. Between 1926 and 1981—gold's glittering period—its price rose by just 5.8 percent per year, or barely half the annualized return on the S&P 500 Index.

Nearly all of the appreciation in gold prices during this century occurred over the 10 years ended in late 1980. Gold prices have gone mostly nowhere both before and after that relatively brief period.

Commodities

Many investors pick commodities as their ticket to instant wealth. In reality, however, a lottery ticket might provide better odds. Even professional investors, armed with sophisticated trading techniques and the latest software programs, have difficulty consistently making money in the commodity pits.

Money magazine once observed that 90 percent of small investors lost both their money and their taste for commodities within four months. Small wonder! Given the speed, volatility, leverage, and pressure inherent in the commodities business, four months could well seem like 10 years.

Fine Art

Fine art has been the one hard-money asset that gives stocks a run for their money, appreciating by more than 12.5 percent annually. But the difficulties in fine-art investing—primarily illiquidity and high fees—may outweigh its advantages. Art that is popular today could prove difficult to sell tomorrow, and transaction costs are usually sizable. Stock investors have the advantage of being able to sell their holdings quickly and for as little as 1 percent per trade through a discount broker.

Real Estate

Even during the postwar period—a time considered by many to be the golden age for land values—unleveraged real estate has been only a mediocre long-term investment.

Unlike businesses, real estate does not produce or create wealth. Values are based on whatever real estate revenue streams can be generated, and those cash flows are a direct result of overall business health. For example, the cost of owning a single-family home is covered by money earned *through a business.* Consequently, businesses have to be more profitable than real estate or else rents couldn't be paid or houses purchased.

If real estate has been a relatively pedestrian performer over time, why do many people believe it to be so profitable? The answer is simple: leveraging, i.e., the potential to make money with borrowed money. Most excess real estate profits are the result of extreme leveraging, particularly when real estate prices are rising rapidly. The downside, of course, is that while paper profits often go up by borrowing, so do potential losses. Many investors have forgotten that real estate prices are also cyclical.

Whenever you are tempted to see real estate as an investment panacea, remember the real estate market in Texas in the 1980s, or in California in the 1990s. Both took major hits, bursting leverage-driven bubbles. If businesses don't do well, neither does real estate. And if businesses are doing well, there is no better way to get your share of that wealth than by owning a diversified basket of stocks.

IMPORTANCE OF TIME

The most important commodity in your investment toolbox is time. Yet time is often undervalued in our fast-paced culture.

Consider the effects of time on growing your financial nest egg (Exhibit 12-2). Over a typical 45-year working lifetime, the difference between a $100,000 investment compounding at 5 percent and at 10 percent (the long-term average for common stocks) is $6.4 million. And the difference between earning 10 percent and 15 percent—a reasonable target for value investors—is $46.5 million over those 45 years. Yes, equity prices will fluctuate, but perhaps tolerating some volatility is well worth any uncertainty over the long haul.

EFFECTS OF INFLATION

Remember 1982, when economists assured us that Paul Volcker had killed the inflation dragon once and for all? That belief proved greatly exaggerated. As long as households,

E X H I B I T   1 2 - 2

The Power of Compound Interest
How a $100,000 investment would grow over various time periods at
different interest rates

Years	Compounding Rate		
	5%	10%	15%
5	$127,628	$ 161,051	$ 201,136
15	207,893	417,725	813,706
30	432,194	1,744,940	6,621,177
45	898,501	7,289,048	53,876,927

corporations, and governments borrow and spend excessively, we remain on course for more inflation and high
interest rates.

Inflation has always been present, though at certain
points in the business cycle it usually remains discreetly out
of sight. Currently, inflation is strictly a monetary phenomenon. The American public has never had the political discipline to keep it in check. Inflation has been likened to living
in a country where nobody speaks the truth.

Has the problem disappeared? Hardly. As recently as
1990, consumer prices rose by over 6 percent. That obliter-
ated any real after-tax returns from holding Treasury bills.

CONCLUSION

Chapter 12 presents solid evidence of the superiority of
common stocks as a long-term investment vehicle. In this
chapter we've also described why equity market outperfor-
mance is inevitable. Businesses (common stocks) create the
wealth of an advanced economy. All other values flow from
that wealth. Corporate bond interest is paid by the cash flow

of businesses; government bond interest is paid by taxes on business wealth. Real estate rents are paid by business cash flow. Art, commodities, and precious metals are purchased with wealth produced by businesses. It follows that businesses, over the long term, must produce higher returns than expenses, i.e., bonds, art, commodities, and real estate.

Some of the greatest opportunities in decades currently await prudent and patient investors. Keep repeating the words of Bernard Baruch: two and two equals four. Numbers don't lie, and real value eventually carries the day. The value investor should constantly keep those concepts in mind when mingling with Wall Street.

NOTES

1. Henry R. Oppenheimer, "A Test of Ben Graham's Stock Selection Criteria," *Financial Analysts Journal* (September–October 1984), p. 68.

2. Henry R. Oppenheimer, "Ben Graham's Net Current Asset Values: A Performance Update," *Financial Analysts Journal* (November–December 1986), p. 40.

13

CHAPTER

Which Way to Invest?

In earlier chapters, we showed why a patient, value-oriented approach to a globally diversified portfolio of common stocks is the best way to invest over the long term. The only remaining question is how to implement that plan.

Value investing can be approached through a variety of methods; none is necessarily better than any other. The choice of method simply reflects personal preference in the way a value strategy is executed.

METHODS OF INVESTING

This chapter addresses some of the practical aspects of value investing, from the nitty-gritty of doing it yourself to employing an investment advisor. We also provide tips on how to get the best results, whichever method you choose. There are four ways to implement a value-investing program:

1. Do it yourself.
2. Use the services of a stockbroker.
3. Invest in mutual funds.
4. Hire an investment advisor.

Of course, a value investor could combine one or more of the methods noted above. Part of the portfolio could be managed personally, while the other portion is invested in mutual funds. Or, if the asset base is large enough, the investor could split funds between a stockbroker and an investment advisor for purposes of comparison. But regardless of which methods the investor chooses, it is vitally important to monitor the results and keep on top of your value program.

Do It Yourself

If you decide to manage your own value portfolio, be aware that it could become an extremely time-consuming process. Serving as your own money manager requires that you do research, monitor executions, and evaluate investment performance. Ideally, do-it-yourself value investors should have considerable experience in portfolio management and accounting. But a value investor with sufficient time and expertise could realistically expect to improve on the returns earned by many professional managers.

The value investor acting independently should plan to spend at least 30 hours a week managing a portfolio. The investor also should subscribe to numerous publications (a listing of information sources is contained in Chapter 3), and send for corporate, annual, and quarterly reports to use in research. The public library can be an important reference tool as well, providing free access to some of the more popular investment publications, including the *Value Line Investment Survey.*

Once you have selected a value company for purchase, there are two ways to execute your trades. You could use either a discount broker or a full service broker who does business at discount rates. Although value investors rarely trade extensively, keeping transaction costs to a minimum can make a substantial difference in your bottom line over the long haul.

Finally, the independent value investor should set a target sell price on each security. When any issue reaches its predesignated price, it should be sold unless company fundamentals indicate the sell price should be changed.

Stockbrokers

Some stockbrokers specialize in value investing and do their jobs well. In fact, several large brokerage firms have created separate value research arms. These brokers and firms are worth considering. One caveat: the investor should never operate blindly. The portfolio's management should be monitored closely to be sure the value philosophy remains consistent and absolute.

Value Mutual Funds

Value mutual funds provide diversification and professional money management that is difficult to obtain for the smaller or average-sized account. Of course, the investor also pays for these advantages. Management fees run around 0.75 percent of mutual fund assets. This, plus other miscellaneous costs, may boost annual expenses to well over 1 percent of the amount invested.

What should an investor look for in a fund? Search for offerings with a well-defined long-term value philosophy, continuity of management, and a good long-term performance record. This type of information is easy to find. Two of the best sources are *Morningstar Mutual Funds* and *Value Line Mutual Fund Survey*. Both publications include long-term track records, managerial histories, and style boxes, which quickly reveal whether a fund uses a value approach to securities selection.

The main drawback of fund investing is the lack of the personal touch. Value portfolios in a mutual-fund format can't be tailored to special preferences and needs. And since the holdings are essentially blind pools, some individuals feel distanced from the businesses in which they are investing.

Investment Managers

Managing a value investment program requires considerable time, experience, hard work, and attention to detail. In this regard, it is no different from other professional endeavors where superior long-term results are demanded.

Individuals can and do succeed in managing their own money, given proper training and experience. But in most cases, the skills of a teacher, doctor, lawyer, or other nonfinancial professional do not necessarily translate to portfolio management. In other words, the specialized skills that build wealth in one profession are not necessarily the same as those needed for successful investing.

Because of the highly specialized nature of portfolio management, many investors might do well to consider the services of a professional advisory firm. The advisor carries out the day-to-day work, following a philosophy and plan agreed to by the client.

Keep in mind that most effective money management firms specialize in a particular approach—i.e., value, growth, large-cap, small-cap, domestic, foreign, or some combination. Look for a firm whose philosophy most closely conforms to your own. In other words, choose the philosophy first and the advisor second. Don't pick out an advisor and then inquire as to his or her investment philosophy.

One final caveat: Be sensitive to how your past experiences might affect the way you interact with an advisor. For example, let's say an advisor compiled a superior long-term track record by purchasing low-P/E, small-capitalization businesses that escaped the attention of most investors. Now suppose a potential client's father once put a substantial amount of family money into a small company that went bankrupt, causing great financial distress. In that case, the investor might be psychologically unprepared for a program geared toward investing in small, unknown companies, especially in periods of market declines.

How to Get the Most from an Investment Advisor

Once a competent advisor has been selected, the investor still has a job to do. A good client can help an advisor to function efficiently.

How can a value investor become a good value client? Above all, understand how implementing the value investment philosophy will impact your returns over the short and long terms.

For example, the Graham & Dodd value approach usually means the purchase of unpopular securities. Bargain levels are difficult to find in securities whose prices are actively moving up, or are already widely recognized as superior businesses.

Therefore, an initial value portfolio, unless purchased just before the start of a bull market, may take time to begin moving upward. Unpopular securities do not become market leaders overnight; usually it takes at least three years before a value portfolio begins to demonstrate its initial intrinsic worth.

Being patient, however, doesn't mean being passive. While you are waiting for the more emotion-based segment of the marketplace to recognize your portfolio's intrinsic value, make certain your advisor is sticking to the value approach. Do not, however, get caught up in such "minu-tiae" as short-term quotes, or even monthly portfolio evalu-ations.

If questions arise about particular holdings, focus on how the company fits the chosen philosophy, and whether the advisor is still "on track." The investor's second respon-sibility as a client is to communicate. Tell the advisor how much money is available for equity investments, how much will be available in the future, and your time horizon. Keep the advisor informed of any changes that might affect your plans. Be aware that large and unexpected capital withdraw-als can disturb investment strategies, especially during mar-ket lows. Finally, let the advisor know of concerns or prob-lems that might affect a long-term contract.

Doing your part to make an advisory relationship work can save time, money, and frustration. Changing advisors increases the amount of time required for the plan to prove itself all over again. Additionally, switching advisors usually results in significant transaction costs as one advisor's posi-tions are sold and another's purchased.

14

CHAPTER

Above All, Be Patient

Throughout this book I've emphasized the many characteristics of the successful value investor, including knowledge, discipline, and attention to minute details. Executing a value approach also requires the courage of one's convictions, since the value investor will almost always be going against popular opinion.

But even with all those necessary ingredients in place, you'll still need perhaps the single most important factor: patience. Often, whether an investment proves successful ultimately comes down to simple patience.

Don't expect to gain financial success overnight. There will be periods when stocks aren't performing well. That is when patience becomes especially important to your long-term success. Don't fidget, don't fuss, don't bail out, don't let your emotions get the better of you, and don't be concerned with day-to-day market fluctuations. The business cycle hasn't been conquered, or even leashed. The preceding pages have described the basic value tools and principles, but knowing and understanding those principles won't be enough unless you also have patience and self-discipline.

The investment risks of the last few years have been substantial. However, the returns for skilled and patient investors have been dramatic. Now there is reason to believe that as good as the long-term investment climate has been, it stands to get even better. We live at a time when the human race is poised to advance farther and faster than at any time in history. Even the substantial financial rewards of the last 50 years—spectacular as they have been—may pale beside those of the next 50 years. The purpose of this book is to show an investor how to capture those rewards.

The value-based strategies are relatively simple. However, no investment strategy should be followed blindly, which is why much of this book has been devoted to explaining why the methods work.

A last caveat: Conventional opinion almost always advocates the popular course. But the reader has already seen that the "Street" is oriented toward short-term results and instant gratification.

As an investor, you must steel yourself to stand apart and defy group thinking. Most successful value investors are individualists who have chosen their own path. So, while the rest of the world rushes to buy great concepts or the latest high flyer, the successful value investor must hang tough and stick to basics.

If you do, I believe you will have a markedly better chance of improving investment performance. All that is required is a disciplined mind, the courage of your convictions—and patience. If you have these qualities, I believe you will find investing in businesses throughout the world a rewarding pursuit.

INDEX

ABOUT THE AUTHOR

Charles H. Brandes is the founder and one of five managing partners of San Diego-based Brandes Investment Partners, L.P., a leading manager of domestic, global and international equity portfolios. Founded in 1974, Brandes Investment Partners manages over $10 billion of assets for institutional and private clients. The firm's portfolios have consistently outperformed the markets throughout its history and have produced results ranked among the top in the world.

Mr. Brandes is responsible for directing the management of the firm and overseeing the investment Committee. Early in his career, Mr. Brandes became an acquaintance of Benjamin Graham, the originator of the value approach to investing. He was able to learn first hand how the "Dean" of value investing discovered bargain securities, and became a disciple of value investing. As a member of the Investment Committee, Mr. Brandes uses his expertise in value investing to guide the portfolio review process. Mr. Brandes is a Chartered Financial Analyst (CFA) and has 29 years of investment experience.